HOLLYWOOD
COLOR PORTRAITS

HOLLYWOOD
COLOR PORTRAITS
JOHN KOBAL

Introduction by CARLOS CLARENS

WILLIAM MORROW AND COMPANY, INC.
NEW YORK   1981

Photographs and captions copyright ©1981 by The Kobal Collection
Introduction copyright ©1981 by Carlos Clarens
Published by Aurum Press Ltd, 11 Garrick Street, London WC2
First published in the United States by William Morrow and Company, Inc.

Library of Congress Catalog Card Number 81-82651
ISBN 0-688-00753-8

Typesetting by Tradespools Ltd, Frome, Somerset
Color separations by Latent Image, London
Designed by Neil H. Clitheroe

Printed in Hong Kong
First Edition
1 2 3 4 5 6 7 8 9 10

Previous page

BING CROSBY

for *The Emperor Waltz*, Paramount, 1948
Photographed by BUD FRAKER

The sets by Hans Dreier and Franz Bachelin were perhaps the most
successful part of Billy Wilder and Bing Crosby's joint venture into
Lubitsch territory with Paramount's lush but listless *Emperor Waltz*.
The film was started in 1946 and released in 1948. Bing Crosby, whose
relaxed style nothing could ruffle, played an American gramophone
salesman who sang his way into the heart of a niece of the Emperor of
Austria.

   Only in a still can a set seem to save a film. Bud Fraker was for forty
years a distinguished stills and portrait photographer at Paramount.
This production shot, typical of his fine work, catches Crosby in his
customary relaxed pose, and does justice to the accumulated wealth
of material and talent which a major studio could easily expend in the
hope of a hit.

For Simon Crocker
whose brainchild this was

Acknowledgments

In at last realizing this long cherished project, I would like to make my appreciation known to the people who helped make it possible: the staff of the Kobal Collection for their valuable comments and suggestions; John Russell Taylor, Bill Gibb, Henry Thoresby, Guillermo Cabrera Infante, and Ted Allan for more of the same; and Mary Corliss, Carlos Clarens, Ben Carbonetta, and Lou Valentino for help with some of the rare, previously unpublished color photographs in this book.

Publisher's Note

Great care has been taken in the reproduction of the photographs in this book, but the delicate and in some cases unstable nature of the original film or transparencies has given rise to occasional, unavoidable blemishes and unevenness of color.

IN GLORIOUS, ELUSIVE, EVERLASTING TECHNICOLOR

It is difficult to conceive, from our viewpoint in the Polaroid age, how elusive color used to be in the first third of the century; and yet photography's obsession with color dates back to its very beginnings. If the parent art of photography evolved and preserved an esthetic and blacks and whites in a world gone deliriously color-happy, the cinema – younger and less mature – adopted realism as a final, absolute aspiration and would not be deterred from acquiring sound, color and relief, although not necessarily in that order: color came to the cinema before sound did, and a viable stereoscopy is still in the future.

The battle for color films never really abated. Primitive filmmakers of the turn of the century had to resort to crude and painstaking techniques such as having individual frames illuminated by hand, like the pages in a medieval manuscript and conveying to the modern viewer a similar archaic charm. There were dozens of patented color processes, some more successful than others, but the real breakthrough in cinema color came as early as 1917 with the invention of the process called additive two-strip Technicolor, which combined two separate negatives – one yellow-red, the other blue-green – to recompose on the screen a limited color spectrum. A complex interplay of financial and technical factors prevented Technicolor from perfecting a more stable three-strip process until 1932. Then, the fate of black-and-white film was sealed by a few Disney Silly Symphonies and a feature, *Becky Sharp*, made and released in 1935. It was only a matter of time – thirty years to be exact – before the industry switched almost entirely to color.

This, in a nutshell, is the history of Technicolor, its power and its glory. It took years to consolidate that power and to achieve the sumptuous visual experience that it strove for. It ran into opposition almost immediately – Graham Greene spoke for the cultural establishment when he declared the first Technicolor efforts 'hideous'. Both defenders and critics of the new process seemed caught in a boyish obsession to have photography supplant reality, and not even Herbert T. Kalmus, the guiding spirit of Technicolor, seemed to be aware that color pictures could be independent works of art.

The Technicolor legend was born in a box-car laboratory in 1917 where Dr Kalmus devised the rudiments of what eventually grew into an awesomely complicated technique. Rather than drowning in detail about the process, let us simplify: a prism split the light beam as it entered the camera, registering the image in two separate strips of film (which eventually became three). The early process was known as additive, and it required special attachments on the projector. Kalmus gradually realized that, to succeed, every step of the work prior to the projection of color film should be done in special laboratories. He set out to design and build cameras that could contain three separate packs of film from which separation matrices would be made. Once soaked in the correct colored dye, the matrices could be combined to produce a perfect Technicolor positive.[1]

The cameras were bulky and the lights required twice as strong as those employed in black-and-white cinematography so that the performers ran the risk of being washed out by light, not to mention sweltering in the heat, which also caused perspiration to show through make-up and costumes. And the final effect was often aberrant, so technique had to advance by trial and error. Lipstick for street wear, for instance, contained a blue pigment that gave a bluish cast to the lips. Before Perc Westmore, head of the make-up department at Warner Brothers, pioneered a pure pigment lipstick (from which a cosmetics industry evolved) the fate of many an established star was in serious doubt.

'This type of color,' contended Eddie Mannix, studio manager at Metro-Goldwyn-Mayer, 'would eventually ruin female stars.' There had been complaints – as it turned out, unfounded – about how badly Joan Crawford appeared in Technicolor, how she burst into tears after seeing herself in a Technicolor sequence for *Ice Follies* (1939), Metro's second attempt at Technicolor. Dr Kalmus was called to account: the prints could be improved for general release, and anyway the star herself, when consulted, admitted that she liked what she saw. What Technicolor could not accomplish, however, was to make Joan Crawford beautiful enough to save a picture as bad as *Ice Follies*, contended Kalmus.[2] The success of *The Wizard of Oz*, that same year, won the argument for Technicolor. A new category for Best Color Cinematography was created by the Academy of Motion Picture Arts and Sciences to reward *Oz* and *Gone with the Wind*.[3]

Technicolor had come to stay, and as more color pictures appeared on the screens of the world, the name of Natalie Kalmus became synonymous with that of the process. Not only did Mrs Kalmus' name appear on the credits of every Technicolor film but she also became spokesperson and roving ambassadress for the company. While Dr Kalmus stayed home, close to the Hollywood plant, keeping a lower profile and ironing out the technical problems that arose, she went off lecturing, making sales contacts in New York (with commercial firms such as Postum, Elizabeth Arden and Wrigley's chewing gum), and as far as London to set up another plant in the hope of enticing British filmmakers to make their films in the three-color process. An early convert was Alexander Korda who in 1936 was already planning a color epic based on the exploits of Lawrence of Arabia, whom recent death had suddenly restored to fame after seventeen years of self-willed obscurity.

Regarded as the first British Technicolor feature, *Wings of the Morning* was in fact processed at the California plant: it barely qualifies as a British product, having been capitalized by 20th Century-Fox with frozen English funds, directed by an American (Harold Schuster), photographed by the pioneer Technicolor cameraman, Ray Rennahan, and starring Hollywood's Henry Fonda and France's Annabella. Nonetheless, the location cinematography in England and Ireland, swathed in a variety of mists, over-ruled the technicalities. And Mrs Kalmus had done her job well: Korda's Lawrence project failed to come off, but three features in his 1938–9 schedule – *The Divorce of Lady X*, *The Drum* and *The Four Feathers* – were made in Technicolor and processed in London, as was a film version of *The Mikado* produced by Gilbert and Sullivan Productions. Needless to say, La Kalmus was credited as color consultant in all of them. She was equally ubiquitous at home where her squad of 'colorists' was being regarded as something of an imposition by directors, set costumes and designers, make-up and prop men, even wardrobe mistresses – and she herself ridiculed as a know-all on the subject of color.[4] Some of Mrs Kalmus' esthetic pronouncements were of course biased: 'The monotony of gray, black and white in comparison with color is an acknowledged fact', she wrote in an essay meant for widespread syndication: 'Lack of color is unnatural', she added with complete disregard for the wholly evolved esthetic of the cinema until then. Her dictates of the physiological and psychological effects of color, rigid and basic as they may now seem, were quite fresh at the time and more than justified by the still unwieldy techniques of Technicolor.[5]

By 1942, in a statement actually ghosted by one Raymond Dannenbaum but carefully copyedited by Mrs Kalmus herself, she imparts sensible advice to the amateur color photographer on 'how to tie color in with the mood of the story.' The same year, she could take justifiable pride in the almost subliminal persuasion of her closely watched color schemes for the movie version of Ernest Hemingway's novel *For whom the Bell tolls*: 'The color has been kept unobtrusive so that it will not break the spell of realism. This parallels the style in which Hemingway writes. The choice of costume colors has not been left to chance because to be truly realistic they had to be as deliberately chosen as if the story had been a fantasy. The warm green shirt which Miss Bergman wears is the freshest note in all the costumes ... And the general O.D. and khaki color ensemble of Jordan's is ... characteristic and similar to the American soldier's uniform ...'[6]

Resented as arrivists in the ever-spreading technology of the cinema, the color consultants had to account in turn to Henri C. Jaffa, Mrs Kalmus' conscientious right-hand man and the head of the aptly titled Department of Color Control at Technicolor. Not even the most minute accessory, the smallest detail, could appear in a Technicolor picture without exhaustive pre-testing. A memo from Mr Jaffa on the subject of Cecil B. De Mille's *Northwest Mounted Police* is quite specific: 'There will also be tests of quicksilver, bullet effects, lucite material for campfire, and cast horses.'[7] The expense seemed so phenomenal at the time that certain lesser studios hesitated to take the plunge.

Whenever advice was disregarded, the results were invariably disappointing and inter-office memos at the Romaine Street plant buzzed with self-congratulation. Vera Zorina, the Norwegian ballerina originally cast in the role of Maria in *For whom the Bell tolls* may have been a casualty of a sudden caprice not to comply with the suggestions laid down by the color consultant: 'I understand that one thing they did not like in the production shooting of Zorina was that her face, hair and blouses were all the same value – this is a point which we made very emphatically to all concerned at the time the blouses were selected and our advice was overlooked by Mr Menzies [production designer] and Mr Wood [director].'[8] Shortly thereafter, Zorina was replaced with Ingrid Bergman, whose complexion was no less Scandinavian, nor more Spanish, but who somehow reaped the rewards of such a chastizing experience.[9]

That Jaffa and his colorists were themselves insecure about their demands is also revealed by inter-office correspondence. To their everlasting professional conscience, mistakes were as dutifully reported as the triumphs. 'A bad tie got on a principal', is a succinct admission of guilt, and one is left to imagine the face of a Ray Milland or a Fred McMurray obscured by an incandescent piece of material. Further down the report comes the reassuring information that the film in question was no studio-made romance but *Anchors Aweigh*, a Warner short of 1940 photographed on location in a San Diego shipyard where non-actors presumably wore their everyday working clothes.[10]

A famous blunder came to be known among Technicolor personnel as 'the affair of the hot white towel'. One of the last studios to make a full-length Technicolor feature, Columbia had planned as early as 1937 to go into color with a biography of the composer Frederic Chopin, titled *A Song to Remember*, and to be directed by the studio's ace director, Frank Capra; but Harry Cohn, the Columbia mini-mogul, had chafed at the added expense of Technicolor and indefinitely postponed the picture. (It was eventually made in 1944, in Technicolor as originally planned but with a different director, Charles Vidor.) In 1940 an adobe town was built in Tucson for an epic Western, *Arizona*, and again Cohn backed out of using Technicolor and proceeded to have it photographed in black and white. Finally Columbia and Technicolor reached an agreement in 1942 whereby the first Columbia color picture would be *Pioneers* (ultimately released as *The Desperadoes*). As usual, great care had been taken to have every bit of clothing pre-dyed to Technicolor specifications, but when a bare-chested Glenn Ford reached for a towel during one scene, it proved to be not off-white as planned but unaccountably 'hot', throwing the actor's complexion off-balance in the shot. A temperamental director to say the least, Charles Vidor had tired of being told what and what not to do, and Cohn had tried to cut corners by dismissing color consultant Morgan Padelford before the film had been wrapped up. This particular memo concludes: 'I do not believe they will make further request to have Morgan's work terminated.'[1]

Opinions clashed most frequently on the matter of realism. To certain directors like Henry Hathaway, the more control was exercized, the less realistic the result was bound to look on the screen. Much feared by cast, crew and color consultants, Hathaway had directed *The Trail of the Lonesome Pine*, Paramount's first Technicolor feature and also the first picture to be shot mostly out of doors, on location far from the sound stages, with a corresponding loss of light control. About to embark on *The Shepherd of the Hills*, a similar outdoor story in 1941, Hathaway laid down the law: this time there would be no spraying of color on the rocks as if Nature and

Marlene Dietrich in *The Garden of Allah* (1936), which made sumptuous use of early Technicolor.

An early Technicolor shot from Katherine Hepburn's screen test for the role of Joan of Arc (RKO, 1934).

centuries of erosion had provided them with the wrong palette; nor would there be patches of color sewn on the drab clothes of his mountain people. 'Even garbage would look beautiful in Technicolor, so keep it plain', were Hathaway's final words, dutifully reported to Mrs Kalmus before the day was over.[12]

The major studios continued to resent the combination of time-consuming techniques and finicky experts, but such was the public's acceptance of color during the War years that diehards capitulated one by one: Columbia in 1942, Universal in 1943, and finally RKO Radio in 1945, after Van Nest Polglase stepped down from his post as head of the art department – Polglase had actively resisted any interference of the colorists since 1939.[13] Even a modest studio like Republic felt compelled to make at least one feature in Technicolor, *I've always loved you* in 1946: the studio overextended itself, the film was not a success and the experience was never repeated.

Technicolor had conquered the industry, squashing the competition that occasionally snatched a small-budget short or a poverty row feature away from them. It was a shortlived reign, though. For years, the Technicolor legal department had served subpoenas on competitors like Tricolor and Cinecolor; now, under the Clayton Act, they were charged with monopolistic practices in a number of anti-trust suits. Dr Kalmus publicly riposted that every magazine in the land had carried information on the basic techniques of Technicolor: 'The only secret knowledge we have is know-how, and you can't break up know-how by court order.'[14]

Nevertheless, the film companies had been waiting for such a moment: for almost fifteen years they had reluctantly accepted a process which obviously diminished studio control over their product. In 1939, after he had committed his studio to make at least three color features a year, Jack L. Warner had told Dr Kalmus: 'If the whole industry is going to color they must operate their own color laboratories, just as they operate their own black and white labs.'[15] And the Motion Picture Producers' Association wasted no opportunity to encourage its members to experiment with Dunning Color, a rival process discreetly developed by Warner Brothers which employed a different technique of combining the three complementary colors – blue and red applied on one side of the film stock, yellow on the other. '[We] are interested in watching for this new method which involves much less shifting to a remote laboratory . . .', reads a circular.[16] Remote indeed! The Technicolor plant at Romaine Street was half an hour's drive from the most distant of the studios, Warner's in Burbank.

Yet it was Dr Kalmus himself who unwittingly caused the eventual demise of the three-strip imbibition process almost as soon as it reached universal acceptance by signing with Eastman Kodak to jointly develop a Monopack system that would dispense with the beam-splitting and the three negatives. Monopack had three color layers in the film stock and could be used in standard black-and-white cameras. The system was tried out in the musical sequences of *Happy Go Lucky* in 1942; two years later, *Lassie Come Home* became the first feature entirely photographed in Monopack. The difference was barely noticeable at the time, since the Technicolor lab could still take time to filter and compensate for variations in color, something they could hardly afford later on when the film industry rushed to Monopack in the early fifties. In due time Ansco and duPont began manufacturing their own brand of Monopack, WarnerColor went with Ansco stock, and 20th Century-Fox became affiliated with DeLuxe Laboratories in New York. There were still impeccable prints being processed in the

London and Rome Technicolor plants. If they now seem the most perfect ever, especially films like *French Can-Can* and *Les Grandes Manoeuvres*, it is also because some of the best European directors, such as Jean Renoir and René Clair, saw fit to reinvent the esthetics of color film rather than abide by any one precept.

It is ironic, but also dramatically fitting, that the Kalmuses, who had presided together over the golden years of Technicolor, would part in 1948 after a bitter court battle in which Mrs Kalmus sued for half of her husband's estate under the California divorce law. Her claim, however, was dismissed when it was revealed that the Kalmuses had originally divorced in 1919 but had kept it a secret even from their close friends, occupying adjoining suites in the same Bel Air address and vacationing together in Cape Cod, where they maintained a summer home. After 1950, the name of Natalie Kalmus disappeared from the screen credits to be replaced by that of the actual color consultant, just another unassuming technician, and in time by that of more illustrious photographers and trendsetters like Elliott Elisofon, George Hoyningen-Huene and Richard Avedon.[17]

In the mid-sixties, after directors like Federico Fellini, Luchino Visconti, Ingmar Bergman and Michelangelo Antonioni had made their color debuts, it was said, rather unfairly, that color cinema had finally reached its maturity. Whoever so pretended was confusing directorial control with technical proficiency. In fact, color had lost not only its novelty but its power to amaze the viewer. Gone were the burnished looks of a film like *Blood and Sand*, the crisp airiness of outdoor adventures like *Northwest Passage*, the cheerful and much maligned candybox effect of the Betty Grable and Rita Hayworth musicals. For nearly two decades, despite the fact that every Technicolor film was processed in one place, the Hollywood studios managed to retain their individuality, their house style – a tribute to the cameramen, art directors and costume designers involved in the visual aspect of a film. The average filmgoer was aware of such continuity and could tell at a glance, if he walked into a theater after the picture had started, whether it came from Paramount, Warner or Universal. Similarly there was a distinct quality to British Technicolor, a certain attractive pallor in skin tones for instance; the reason being that, even if the color dyes were the same as those used in America, the quality of a basic solvent like water was not.

The Kalmus process, and the unstinting professionalism of the firm's employees, was vindicated for ever when a spotcheck of the prints deposited in the Library of Congress in Washington revealed that most color films produced after 1953 had either 'turned red' or faded beyond retrieval; but not those in three-strip imbibition Technicolor. In order to reduce costs, Eastman tints had an organic base susceptible to change under the influence of time, storage conditions and the heat of the projector's arc acting on the filmstrip as it unspooled. Kalmus, on the other hand, had made sure that only printer's inks were used, their durability having been known in the art world since the days of the great engravers. Like Toulouse-Lautrec's printing house, Technicolor had in fact worked for posterity, and to the string of adjectives usually appended – 'glorious!' being the most often used – we can now add 'everlasting'.

We never saw Garbo on the color screen, but a few rare on-the-set color shots survive to stir our imagination. As faithful chroniclers of the film world, fan magazines began to use color almost in unison with the studios, having a few on-the-set transparencies made in Kodachrome or Ektachrome, even if the film itself was being photographed in black and white. At the time there was no precise market for them since color sections were prohibitively expensive and reserved mostly for

ads. Luckily there were also rotogravure pages in the Sunday papers and in the mid-section of fan magazines where color stills could be reproduced in a pleasant bichrome.

Still photography was in fact emulating the industry's transition to color, and to accommodate the new demand a number of publications had to be created. *Life* magazine started publication in 1936, to be followed by *Look*, *Pic*, *Click* and other imitators. A year later, the first 'natural color' cover appeared in *Photoplay*, a portrait of Ginger Rogers by James N. Doolittle.[18] Soon after every studio had its own color gallery, independent of the black-and-white still department, and the few existing 8 × 10 color-plate cameras were being passed from one photographer to another. The technical quality of the transparencies was excellent from the start but their reproduction left much to be desired. Only now can we fully appreciate them, and there is an added pleasure in realizing that color, then regarded as an unrealistic medium, actually conveys as much information as monochrome.[19]

The plates in this book are the work of a dedicated group of photographers whose mastery of black and white did not prevent their experimenting with color. Edwin Bower Hesse and James N. Doolittle were among the first ever to take color portraits of the stars, and they were soon followed by Frank Powolny, Ernest Bachrach, Scotty Welbourne, and Ted Allan.[20] Already famous in the field of black-and-white portraiture, Clarence Sinclair Bull and George Hurrell were quick to adapt their styles to color.

The skeptic or the purist may still wonder whether it was worth so much effort and expense simply to make film audiences color-conscious. After all, the silent cinema was mostly monochrome and the lack of color did not prevent Griffith, Chaplin and Eisenstein from achieving films that even now rank as milestones in the development of twentieth-century art. Ah yes, but as soon as they could, they too availed themselves of color (Griffith, as early as 1921, for *Dream Street*, von Stroheim for *The Wedding March*, Chaplin for his swansong, *The Countess from Hong Kong*, and Eisenstein for *Ivan the Terrible*; they too dreamt in color).

There is a charming moment in Michael Powell's British fantasy *A Matter of Life and Death* (1946) in which a celestial messenger finds himself in a lushly colored Earth after eons in a monochromatic limbo and sighs: 'Heaven is starved for Technicolor.' So was Earth, it seems.

Carlos Clarens

Previous page

GRETA GARBO and ROBERT TAYLOR

Camille, MGM, 1936   **Photographed by FRANK GRIMES**

One of only four color stills cameras in Hollywood belonged to MGM, where Clarence Sinclair Bull took the first color portraits of Greta Garbo in costume for her role as Marguerite Gautier in *Camille*. Ted Allan, who shot Jean Harlow's portraits and those of many of the younger stars, took color costume studies of Elizabeth Allan and Robert Taylor for this film, and stills man Frank Grimes (who alternated with Milton Brown in taking the stills on nearly all Garbo's films) took a number of production and scene stills of *Camille* with the color camera. This rare production shot was found by Mary Corliss, the stills librarian of the Museum of Modern Art[1]; it was taken during a rehearsal between Garbo and Taylor for one of the film's love scenes, with director George Cukor and Garbo's longtime cameraman William Daniels on the far left. The film itself was shot in black and white.

[1] This picture could have been taken on Dufay film, which preceded Eastman's Kodachrome.

NOTES

1   The most readable and comprehensive information on the history of Technicolor is James L. Limbacher's *Four Aspects of the Film* (Brussel & Brussel, New York, 1968).

2   The *Ice Follies* controversy is discussed in a letter from Dr Kalmus to George F. Lewis, board member of Technicolor, 25 April 1939.

3   In the Academy Award ceremony in which *Gone With The Wind* received an Oscar for Best Color Cinematography, William Cameron Menzies received a plaque, Winton Hoch (of Technicolor) a citation, and Technicolor itself a statuette.

4   For the record the original group of color consultants were: Henri Jaffa, William Fritzsche, Robert Brower, Richard Mueller, Morgan Padelford, Monroe Burbank and William Staudigl. Each was assigned to an individual production but could be switched to another if the situation so demanded or if incompatibility arose with studio personnel.

5   'Color Photography' by Natalie M. Kalmus, 1935.

6   'The Black and White of Color Photography' by Natalie M. Kalmus, 1942.

7   Memo from Henri Jaffa to staff, 12 February 1940.

8   Memo to Mrs Kalmus from Henri Jaffa, 30 July 1942.

9   A rumor persists that Menzies' attitude was meant to bring about Zorina's replacement with Bergman, an actress under contract to David O. Selznick, a former employer of Menzies.

10   Memo from Henri Jaffa, 17 August 1940.

11   Memo to Mrs Kalmus from Henri Jaffa, 30 July 1942.

12   Letter to Mrs Kalmus from Henri Jaffa, 17 August 1940.

13   Wanter Wanger had produced *Arabian Nights* on the Universal lot in 1942, but the first official Universal Technicolor feature was *White Savage* in 1943. Likewise, International Pictures used some of RKO Radio's personnel and facilities in two Technicolor features, *Belle of the Yukon* and *It's a Pleasure*, but it was *The Spanish Main* in 1945 which marked the studio's first direct commitment with Technicolor.

14   Quoted in *Current Biography*, February 1949.

15   Letter from Dr Kalmus to George F. Lewis, 25 April 1939.

16   Letter from the MPPAA, 1 November 1938. (The Lincoln Center Library for the Performing Arts, New York.)

17   Dr Kalmus retained the presidency of Technicolor Inc. until his retirement in 1960. He died in 1963. Mrs Kalmus died in 1965.

18   Doolittle used a home-made Devin type 'one shot' camera for his cover shots. This camera made three 5 × 7 color separation negatives, and Carbro prints were made from them.

19   The 8 × 10 transparencies in Dufay Color, an early English process, were shot with the same camera and film holders as black-and-white pictures. Dufay Color had a microscopic screen or grid that consisted of squares of the primary colors. During exposure, the color photographed would 'reveal itself' to the corresponding color on the grid and become transparent.

20   Allan built his own sliding-back variety of color camera that changed the film three times during the exposure, which required a frozen position for at least one second. The pictures were printed by Eastman Dye-Transfer from Wash-Off-Relief film.

The author wishes to express his gratitude to Ronald Haver, of The Los Angeles County Museum, for making available a limited but indispensable part of the Technicolor archives. Also to Eric Spilker for his advice on technical matters.

W.C. FIELDS

Mississippi, Paramount, 1934
Photographed by PAUL HESSE

W.C. Fields in one of the series of special color portraits taken for Paramount's 1934 service manuals. The costume is for his co-starring role in the 1935 Bing Crosby musical, *Mississippi*.

The actor-screenwriter, born William Claude Dukenfield in 1879 (died 1946), began his celebrated stage career with the ambition of becoming the world's foremost juggler, and went on to become a cult figure for his collection of sincerely felt braggarts, drunkards, misogynists and misanthropes – characters which, since he also wrote most of his scripts, took a large dose of their authenticity from the bitter experiences of his own life. His reputation for not suffering animals, women, children gladly (as well as bankers, lawyers, accountants, Baby LeRoy and Mae West among others) was all quite true. If women held back in their admiration, men did not; many shared his gripes and agreed with the summing up of one of Field's friends that, 'Any man who hates small dogs and children can't be all bad.'

MAE WEST

Belle of the Nineties, Paramount, 1934
Photographed by PAUL HESSE
Costume by TRAVIS BANTON
Set by HANS DREIER and BERNARD HERZBRUN

Mae West (born 1892, died 1980) in costume for her 1934 box office triumph *Belle of the Nineties*. Begun as *That St Louis Woman*, based on an original story and screenplay by Mae West, it was initially advertized as *It Ain't No Sin* but finally released under the less controversial title of *Belle of the Nineties* to deflect the moral crusaders who had already fumed and raged at earlier examples of her wonderfully bawdy wit and earthy wisdom, and for whom this gloriously funny woman symbolized society's worst excesses. In this film, in this gown, on this set, accompanied by Duke Ellington and his band, she introduced the standard 'My Old Flame' – a rare contemplative moment for a woman not given to reminiscing. (It was the only memorable thing she didn't write herself, but nobody since has ever sung quite so well.)

> Approaching the spectacle
> And wit of Mae West
> Awe is everything
> Silence, the rest.

CLAUDETTE COLBERT

as *Cleopatra*, Paramount, 1934
Photographed by PAUL HESSE

Of the many screen incarnations of the romantically foolish, politically shrewd Egyptian queen, this was Cecil B. DeMille's. His Victorian puritan's approach to the sex and scandals surrounding Cleopatra's throne reflected her continuing appeal to the imagination – even if that imagination were really a childhood fantasy of adult desires. Authenticity, except as decorative embroidery, took second place to his desire to capture her timeless appeal on film. Facts and figures may vary, fashions and desirable objects may be ever changing, but sex, sin and punishment make up a triangle of eternal allure. (A point which the much more costly, authentically reconstructed, historically truthful 1963 version completely missed.) Travis Banton's wardrobe transformed Claudette Colbert from a coy star into a splendid, shimmering siren – a seductive ikon – and, with fanciful art direction by Hans Dreier and Roland Anderson, the film had the opulence, the barbarity, the epic sweep and shocking decadence of certain books and paintings that were at the heart of so much of this film: the brothers Grimm, the Arabian Nights, Alma-Tadema and Holman Hunt. This rare and beautiful portrait was one of a series taken by Paul Hesse of Paramount stars for the studio's annual publicity manual, to help its salesmen sell the year's products to the distributors.

The French-born, American-raised Claudette Colbert made three films with Cecil B. DeMille, but felt more comfortable in contemporary comedies, for one of which (*It Happened One Night*, 1934) she won an Oscar and in all of which she identified herself with the most American of American secretaries, sweethearts, wives and mothers. Her popularity lasted well into the fifties; her magic rests with Cleopatra.

MARLENE DIETRICH

Angel, Paramount, 1937
Photographed by DON ENGLISH
Costume by TRAVIS BANTON

Marlene Dietrich in costume for her last film under contract to Paramount, *Angel*, directed by Ernst Lubitsch.

Dietrich was the human face of Garbo, making trousers fashionable, mystery accessible, grandmothers glamorous and time stand still. Born in Berlin in 1901, she made her first film in 1923, and her last to date in 1978. In between she was always in the middle of the action: in the Berlin theatrical and cabaret life of the twenties; Hollywood of the thirties; battlefronts of World War II; and in her triumphant one-woman show which swept through the theaters and music halls of the world from the fifties on into the early seventies; she was a staggering creature embodying illusion, survival and protest – an indelible part of this century's cultural landmarks. And all she originally wanted to be was a good violinist.

DOROTHY LAMOUR

The Hurricane, United Artists, 1937
Photographed by ALEX KAHLE

Dorothy Lamour as Marama of the Isle of Manukura being prepared for her wedding to Terangi, in Samuel Goldwyn's 1937 disaster epic, *The Hurricane*, directed by John Ford. The photograph is by RKO's still and portrait artist Alex Kahle, one of the few photographers Ford would allow on his sets, and the man responsible for most of the memorable still images from Ford's films, as well as those directed by Orson Welles.

Dorothy Lamour, born Mary Leta Dorothy Kaumeyer, was a beauty queen, elevator operator, band singer and radio personality before becoming an overnight film star, at the age of twenty-two, in *The Jungle Princess* (Paramount, 1936); the film launched her career and defined her image for ever more as a long-haired child of the Islands who wore fancy tablecloths. She was a full-lipped brunette charmer, well suited to smoky nightclubs, Caribbean entanglements and oriental chicanerie. Moonlight became her – it went with her hair – and if daylight was less discriminating, she was still light-hearted, good-natured, breezy and decorative, and her career took on added longevity when she was cast in the popular series of 'Road' comedies where she played Margaret Dumont to Crosby and Hope.

GLORIA SWANSON

MGM, 1937
Photographed by CLARENCE SINCLAIR BULL

Gloria Swanson in a portrait study from a fashion spread in *Photoplay* magazine. Although at this time she hadn't appeared in a film for several years and wasn't to make one for several more, Gloria Swanson remained a presence in the Hollywood of the thirties, the only legendary silent star to sustain an image and continue to interest the film studios, which put her under contract and announced her to star in a series of projects – none of which were realized. While she wasn't to regain her former eminence until her celebrated comeback as Norma Desmond in Billy Wilder's *Sunset Boulevard*, a scathing satire on Hollywood and the self-delusions of its former heroes, she maintained her silent-screen image as the personification of glamour, and as such wasn't the initial choice for the role of the faded silent star.

Like many small people who achieve greatness, Swanson, born in 1899 and barely five feet tall, was a powerhouse of energy, vitality, ambition and shrewdness, untroubled by insight or humor to slow down her pace. She made her first film appearance in 1913, in a short produced in her native Chicago, and had her last starring role to date in *Airport 1975* (Universal, 1974). The key to her success, the charm of her personality, the glamor of her career and the secret of her survival was superbly captured by herself in one of the best autobiographies of recent years, *Swanson on Swanson*. Its triumph had the assurance and surprise that made her so intriguing in all her efforts.

ANN SOTHERN

RKO Radio, 1937
Photographed by ERNEST BACHRACH

Harriet Lake, as good a name as any other for a future star, began her film career in 1929, but changed her name to Ann Sothern when she returned from Broadway in 1933 to become the sophisticated leading lady in B comedies. Her real popularity came under still another name, as *Maisie* (1939), the bouncy blonde, scatterbrained heroine of ten features made between 1939 and 1947; and in the fifties, she found a perfect showcase for her brand of warm humor in two popular TV series: *Private Secretary* and *The Ann Sothern Show.* Always an energetic performer, she was still active in films as a character actress in the late seventies.

Overleaf
GRETA GARBO
and CHARLES BOYER

Conquest, MGM, 1937
Photographed by FRANK GRIMES

Greta Garbo and Charles Boyer as Marie Walewska and Napoleon during a public moment of their private affair in the 1937 historical romance *Conquest.* Most of the color stills and portraits from the thirties were of films made in black-and-white and their actual purpose was limited. The color range of this one, for instance, does not fully express the work of the craftsmen involved since the set was not lit to bring out the kodachromatic range of the stars' wardrobe by Adrian or the art direction supervised by Cedric Gibbons. The standing of these men, both of whom worked at MGM, was as high in their profession as that of the stars whose appeal they served. As was only to be expected with a studio which had built its reputation upon its star power, the sets and costumes for their 'vehicles' were of an importance almost equal with that of the director and the story, and when the 'vehicle' was harnessed to the right star their contribution could camouflage most other defects. Yet clothes do not a character make nor palaces a plot, and by 1937 Metro's script department was showing frantic signs of the problems it had in finding suitable stories for the industry's most prestigious star – who was slowly but surely turning into a white elephant. Ever since *Queen Christina*, Garbo's broad public support had dwindled. *Camille* had the critics, but not the cinemagoers, in a daze. *Conquest* – which might have been livened up by color – was an attempt by all departments to secure a hit. Garbo's co-star was the romantic idol of the day, Charles Boyer; the subject was to have an epic sweep – Napoleon's retreat from his disastrous Russian campaign, through Poland and Marie Walewska, on his inevitable way to Elba; Garbo's role – as his suffering, cast-off mistress, victim of high politics – was a chance to touch the heartstrings. It all failed, for reasons clearly laid out early on in the story when Marie tells an admonitory Emperor: 'Sire. You stand in the sun.' Garbo's fans saw no point in their idol standing in the shadows.

JEANETTE MacDONALD

for *Maytime*, MGM, 1937
Photographed by CLARENCE SINCLAIR BULL

Jeanette MacDonald was the deliciously sophisticated star of twenty-eight films, from her debut in Lubitsch's first sound film, *The Love Parade* (Paramount, 1929), to one of the best of the 'Lassie' series, *The Sun Shines Bright* (MGM, 1949). A singer in all of them, she communicated effortless ease, sincerity and sparkling humor – qualities she refined in her four films with the master of the light touch, Ernst Lubitsch, and brought with her to relieve the antiquated operettas which took much of their fresh appeal from her presence. If the critics did not give her her due, failing to see the wood for the trees, her enduring public support ensures her lasting fame as one of the great idols of thirties' films, especially for the series of eight opulently remounted musicals which co-starred her with Nelson Eddy. They began with *Naughty Marietta* (1934), and were scored by Victor Herbert, Rudolf Frimml, Sigmund Romberg, as well as Noël Coward and Rodgers and Hart.

This casual study was made between takes for one of the best in the series, *Maytime*, at MGM, where she worked exclusively between 1934 and 1942. The costume was by the celebrated Adrian.

JAMES STEWART

MGM, 1937
Photographed by TED ALLAN

James Stewart, the Princeton-educated actor, was a sexy man when he
made his film debut as a gawky gangly shy backwoods type in the mid-
thirties, and was still as sexy, though more complex, as the neurotic
hero of enormously popular Westerns and thrillers directed by men
like John Ford and Alfred Hitchcock in the late forties and fifties. Born
in 1908, he made his first film in 1935, and starred in his last film to
date in 1978 – the family picture *The Magic of Lassie*. He has won
countless acting awards, popularity polls, a fortune in percentages
from shrewdly selected box office hits, and the rank of brigadier
general in the US Air Force Reserve. This picture dates from the first
phase of his screen career, before such perennial classics as *Destry
Rides Again*, *You Can't Take It With You*, *Mr Smith Goes To
Washington*, *Philadelphia Story* and *Shop Around The Corner*.

LORETTA YOUNG

20th Century-Fox, 1938
Photographed by FRANK POWOLNY

Loretta Young is a phenomenon whose long and popular career poses a problem when it comes to assessing her place in the Hollywood pantheon. Neither her sincerity as an actress, nor her rapturous starry-eyed beauty can really account for her longevity nor explain her positive influence, over the years, on her fans. Her career spanned almost forty years from 1917 as a four year old child extra to her last starring role in a film in 1953. Although she starred in many successful films, and even won an Oscar in 1947 for her performance as a Swedish housekeeper in *The Farmer's Daughter*, she was never a star who had a great role to call her own – a Gilda, a Laura, a Rebecca or a Jezebel, for example. Not until 1953 that is, when as the star of *The Loretta Young Show* she found the vehicle that made her one of the greats. The remarkable fact that she could come across as such a refreshing surprise, be re-discovered as it were after four decades in the public eye, was the result of her steady if unspectacular approach to her career. She could have risked making the quantum leap from being a popular leading lady to becoming a superstar in 1939, the year she broke her long-term contract with 20th Century-Fox. It wasn't that she lacked the ability or the desire to shock, but when the opportunity came, her need for it was not there. Instead, she skilfully continued to refine her craft and hold on to her popularity. By the time she played off-beat roles in films like *Rachel and the Stranger*, or Orson Welles' *The Stranger*, she was in fact too familiar to really surprise, for she had elected to develop her career along the lines of a dancer or a craftsman whose talent, always there, only comes into its own after a period of time has passed, when it is suddenly realized that she is still there, still turning out beautiful stuff. It took the change of medium to do this. The small screen revealed her size. Now her ability, long overlooked, to adapt herself to suit many different roles came into its own. And with that she became an institution, one of the most famous women in America. As talented at business as she was at her craft, she had long ago seen through those who judged her only by her fragile china beauty, and she successfully outmanoeuvred and outlasted not only most of her contemporaries, but also some of the shrewdest producers in the business. Her way had paid off.

GARY COOPER

The Westerner, United Artists, 1940
Photographed by BOB COBURN

While Cooper's career spanned ninety-two feature films, in which he appeared as everything from a masked cossack to an Italian Renaissance explorer, a foreign legionnaire, a baseball great and countless sophisticated romantic adventurers, he is best remembered as a Western star. In *The Westerner*, a character drama directed by William Wyler revolving around Judge Roy Bean's obsession with Lily Langtry, Cooper played Cole Hardin, a drifter who wry-talks his way out of problems. Cooper and his old cohort, Walter Brennan, had a field day in the main roles, with Brennan becoming the first person to win an Oscar for Best Supporting Actor for a third time. It was another Western, the seminal classic *High Noon* (1952), that won Cooper the second of his own two Oscars, the first being for his performance as baseball's hero, Lou Gehrig, in *Pride of the Yankees*. Twenty years after his death, the screen has found no replacement for him.

Overleaf
ELEANOR POWELL

on set for the finale of *Broadway Melody of 1938*, MGM, 1937
Photographed by ED CRONENWERTH
Art direction by CEDRIC GIBBONS
Sets by EDWIN B. WILLIS
Tuxedo (Miss Powell's trademark) by ADRIAN

'I'd rather *dance* than eat!' Eleanor Powell said it, and meant it. On film, as in conversation, she *was* energy. In the heyday of her musicals, from 1935 to 1942, the studio built ever bigger Everests for her spectacular dance numbers – battleships, mountains of drums, acres of mirrors that stretched from one soundstage into another – over all of which her energy flowed in steps strong, fast, hard, close to the ground, an endless wave of brilliant taps, beating out a Reveille to Life. No set dwarfed her, no number, however complex and strenuous she could make it, exhausted her; the effect was always one of elation. Her efforts went into dreaming up new ways to top herself.

The greatest female dancing star in films, Powell had taken up dancing when still a child to help overcome her awful shyness. It was that drive which also made her such a compelling star. She made her Broadway debut in 1929 and her film debut in 1935; only twenty-three, she was already one of MGM's superstars. For the next seven years the studio came up with plots that would allow her to tap. Less was done to use her other great assets: sincerity, honesty, and in everything except dancing, true modesty. She reached straight to the heart, ensuring that her achievement was never isolated but always personal; the public rooted for her success, and felt pride in her triumph.

While it seemed more difficult to find a suitable partner who would not be eclipsed by her than would have been the case for her male colleagues, her one teaming with Fred Astaire, in *Broadway Melody of 1940*, became a celebrated meeting of peers; when they seguied into Cole Porter's 'Begin the beguine' both the stars and the musical came together for one of its finest moments.

VIVIEN LEIGH

Off the set for *Gone With The Wind*, MGM, 1939
Photographed by FRED PARRISH

In the book *The Dream of the Red Chamber*, there's a magical stone, which at one point snaps back at the constant demands to explain itself with: 'What do you mean, what do I mean! I'm a stone!' The British actress Vivien Leigh might have vented her exasperation at similar demands by us with: 'What do you mean, what do I mean! I'm Vivien Leigh!' Born in Britain in 1913, Vivien Leigh made her film debut in 1934, played Scarlett O'Hara in 1939 and died of tuberculosis in 1967, long after people still died of this obsolete illness. But then, this extraordinary star, unsentimental, detached, neither asking nor giving nor expecting sympathy for herself or her characters (the two being far more interchangeable than anyone ever suspected), was nothing if not contrary. She was predestined to make her mark in something as sprawling and epic as a *Gone With The Wind*, for only in the midst of so much *sturm und drang* would her precise articulate self-control and emotional coolness receive its due. While all around were losing their heads, she kept hers. And it's no surprise that she should get some of her worst reviews for her finest performance as *Anna Karenina*, for she was Tolstoy's foolish, self-indulgent, anti-romantic heroine to perfection. When the train came, under it was the only place to go. No tears for such logic. Highly undervalued by the English critics – what other actress was as capable as she of speaking the most profound and lengthy text at so rapid a pace, with such brilliant clarity, and without spittle? – it took the camera to get to the heart of this woman, and make the need that drove this lovely, lonely spirit all the more appealing for asking nothing for itself except to be allowed to get on and do her work. She won two Oscars for her work.

LANA TURNER

1939 (un-retouched)
Photographed by LASZLO WILLINGER

By the time this early portrait was taken of pretty redheaded Julia Jean Turner from Idaho, she had already come a long way. Three years before, at the counter of Top's Cafe at Sunset and Highland (not, as myth perpetuates, at Schwab's) the publisher of *The Hollywood Reporter* had spotted her, and that sighting had led to a contract with producer-director Mervyn LeRoy; the role in his film created a furore which made it clear that hers were ingredients for stardom. The precocious seventeen year old's five-minute part was that of a nubile, high-school murder victim in Warner Brothers' courtroom drama *They Won't Forget* (1937). Her brief appearance, like that of Harlow in *Hell's Angels* and Monroe in *Asphalt Jungle*, had an impact far beyond its length, and made the sweater she wore a symbol of feverish sexuality, sweeping it into vogue throughout America. Columnist Walter Winchell, who also coined 'oomph' to describe Ann Sheridan's asset, dubbed Lana 'America's Sweater Girl Sweetheart'. Suddenly every young girl wished she could look like her, and her boyfriend wished she could too.

In 1938 LeRoy took Lana with him to MGM, where she was groomed to fill the slot Jean Harlow had left vacant with her death, and stayed till the late fifties as one of that studio's proudest accomplishments. Yet its success was not in making her a star – the public had done that – but in turning her potential into one of the most enduring, glamorous careers. Early on in her contract, the studio had considered dropping her as a risky proposition because of the frequency with which she made dubious headlines, but the public, having chosen her, continued to support her. Box office reports on her films continued to climb. Whatever the problems the headstrong teenager might cause the publicity department, it clearly had no effect on her popularity. MGM's czar, Louis B. Mayer, gave the go-ahead for the final stage in her elevation to stardom: her hair was dyed blonde, her roles were tailored, the brashness balanced by come-uppance, and in the lavish *Ziegfeld Girl* (1941), co-starring Judy Garland, Hedy Lamarr and James Stewart, it was Lana, as the happy-go-lucky, doomed showgirl, who walked away with the picture. Over the next fourteen years and eight husbands, the studio's decision to keep her proved to be the right one.

JUDY GARLAND
and MICKEY ROONEY

Strike Up The Band, MGM, 1940
Photographed by ERIC CARPENTER

Frances Gumm (born 1922) of the singing Gumm sisters, and Joe Yule Jnr (born 1920), son of vaudevillians, who made his film debut playing a midget in a 1926 short. Together in nine films, beginning with *Thoroughbreds Don't Cry* (MGM, 1937), they became one of the most popular box office teams; *Strike Up The Band* was their fifth. Between them they were married fourteen times but never to each other. The endless public dramas of Garland's woeful public life lent the sort of autobiographical color to her performances that made her a legend in her own time and a cult when she died in 1969. Her death was the last stop in a life which – like that of another screen legend, Marilyn Monroe – had grown to depend ever more on pills for its momentum.

Today Rooney, who was a child star, a musical great and at one point the most popular box office star in America, has survived his own personal and career upheavals (one of his films also featured Marilyn Monroe), to find popularity in character roles after a triumphant return to Broadway as an old-time vaudevillian comic, bringing him success by returning him to his roots.

MARIA MONTEZ

as Scheherazade in *Arabian Nights*, Universal, 1942
Photographed by ROMAN FREULICH
Sets by ALEXANDER GOLITZEN
Costumes by VERA WEST

After her adoring audience had grown up, they discovered that Maria Africa Vidal de Santo Silas (born 1920, died 1951) hadn't done her own singing (she was dubbed), nor her own dancing; her ability as an actress was also put into question, but her spell was not tarnished. Maria Montez was still the madly glamorous South American 'Queen of Technicolor'. What her roles (all of them variations of Scheherazade in slumberland) required were ingredients she had a surplus of: statuesque bearing, regal demeanor, fiery beauty and, best of all, an unassailable confidence in herself. When one weighed all the things she couldn't do against the thing she did so well, the balance came out in her favor. This color shot is from *Arabian Nights* which launched her career. She is about to dance for the cruel sultan, to save the life of her beloved. Her dancing was dubbed.

Overleaf

OLIVIA DE HAVILLAND

JOAN FONTAINE

Santa Fe Trail, Warner Brothers, 1940
Photographed by SCOTTY WELBOURNE
Costume by ORRY-KELLY

1940
Photographed by JOHN MIEHLE

Joan Fontaine (born Joan de Havilland, 1917) and Olivia de Havilland (born 1916) are sisters. De Havilland made her screen debut when Max Reinhardt adapted his stage production of *A Midsummer Night's Dream* to the screen for the 1935 Warner Brothers' film, and brought her to Hollywood to repeat her role. Fontaine made her debut the same year at MGM, as Joan Burfield, playing a minor role in a Joan Crawford picture. She returned to films in 1937 as Joan Fontaine – in order, she says, not to trade on her established sister's famous name. Both sisters had their chance to escape from supporting roles and make their breakthrough as important forties' stars in two films produced by David O. Selznick. Olivia de Havilland – by now typed on screen as Errol Flynn's beautiful, romantic opposite in period swashbucklers – gave a superb performance in the difficult role of Melanie in *Gone With The Wind* (1939), a role her sister had turned down. Fontaine scored her big success in *Rebecca* (1940). At that point in their careers, either girl could have played the other's roles, including the parts that made them famous, but Fontaine was the first to win an Oscar, for her second film with Hitchcock, *Suspicion*. De Havilland won two Oscars, for her roles in *To Each His Own* (1946), and three years later, in *The Heiress*. At the top of her profession, de Havilland began to intersperse films with marriages and theater, and threw away her momentum. Her periodic appearances in the fifties conveyed a decided lack of interest on her part. Meanwhile, her sister also seemed to have lost interest halfway through the forties, becoming increasingly brittle, sophisticated and apparently superior to her work, which took on a grace-and-favor relationship with her audience.

   The two women were beautiful, talented, and for a time, very popular, and never let anyone forget they were sisters through a series of famous feuds with each other.

DOUGLAS FAIRBANKS Jnr

As Mario in *The Corsican Brothers*, United Artists, 1941
Photographed by TOM EVANS

In roles strongly reminiscent of those that made his energetic, dapper, athletic father one of the legendary silent superstars, Fairbanks Jnr played both the twin brothers, Lucien and (portrayed here) Mario Franchi, in Alexander Dumas' *The Corsican Brothers*. If he was never as famous as his father, or his contemporaries, in similar roles, he was nonetheless an engaging, likeable leading man who starred in numerous swashbuckling *Boys Own* adventure stories. And, in his early days as the heir of Pickfair, he made Joan Crawford his Crown Princess on her climb to becoming Queen Bee.

Fairbanks' affection for all things English (he produced and starred in a number of films in England during the thirties and again during the fifties) made him the most English of Americans, in contrast to Cary Grant, the most American of Englishmen. In 1941, he answered the call to real action and as a lieutenant commander in the US Navy participated in several Anglo-American operations for which he was honored by both countries. After the war, he returned to filming and while many of his erstwhile contemporaries have retired or long since faded from the scene, Fairbanks is still a dashing, dapper and debonair performer on stage and in films for TV.

BETTE DAVIS

The Little Foxes, RKO, 1941
Photographed by GEORGE HURRELL

Bette Davis, the most starry of actresses, the most actressy of stars, was the first woman to win two Oscars, for *Dangerous* (Warner Brothers, 1935) and *Jezebel* (Warner Brothers, 1938). She was nominated for many others and deserved most of them. She made her first film in 1931, only to be dropped soon after by the studio for lacking sex appeal, and went on to become the most acclaimed and admired actress of her generation. She has never considered herself a beauty, though many of the great screen beauties would disagree and Graham Greene wrote of her 'corrupt and phosphorescent prettiness'. As famous for her feuds with studio heads, directors, and co-stars as for her courage and integrity, she made the best case for herself in her superb autobiography, *A Lonely Life*, and after fifty years at the top, still works steadily, the finest all-round dramatic star Hollywood has produced.

George Hurrell, the master of glamour photography, with a temperament to complement hers, took numerous celebrated portraits of Davis in his three years at Warner Brothers. This shot of her, in a costume by Orry-Kelly, was taken for her role as Regina Giddens, when she was on loan to Samuel Goldwyn for his 1941 production of *The Little Foxes*; it typifies her compelling stance, her physical appeal, Hurrell's artistry, and the success of her collaboration with the photographer.

HUMPHREY BOGART

Warner Brothers, 1942
Photographed by BERT SIX

The year before this elegant, untypical portrait of Bogart was taken, he had moved from ten years of playing second lead losers – hoods who whined and winced – to stardom as John Huston's wry, neatly groomed private eye, Sam Spade, in *The Maltese Falcon* (WB, 1941). A last-minute casting reshuffle made him a *great* star when he was teamed with Ingrid Bergman (instead of Dennis Morgan with Hedy Lamarr, or Ronald Reagan with Ann Sheridan) in *Casablanca* (WB, 1942). Would Ilsa's memories of Paris, and the song she shared with the man she loved and left the day the Nazis came to town, have meant as much if Rick, the white-tuxedoed romantically disillusioned owner of the Cafe Americaine, had been Morgan or Reagan or any man except Bogart? It took a scruffier part – as the treacherous gold-miner in *The Treasure of the Sierra Madre* (WB, 1949), when he was beaten and balding and had no woman around to bring out his chivalry – to give this star serious recognition as an actor. But the essence of Bogart's glamour, first revealed in *The Maltese Falcon*, lay in his attitude – world-weary, used, tolerant of others as long as they left him and his friends alone – and in a physique that underlined the unimportance of youth and strength. This was something of a revelation in the American perception of romantic masculinity (surprisingly he also succeeded with Europeans, to whom this type of star was after all no novelty) and made him the symbol of a new kind of twentieth-century anti-hero. These inherent traits served him well in the roles he is best remembered for: *High Sierra*, *To Have And Have Not* (which introduced him to his fourth and last wife, Lauren Bacall), *The Big Sleep*, *In A Lonely Place*, and *The African Queen*. It was for the last of these films, released late in his career in 1951, that Bogart received an Oscar – appreciation at last for the originality of this vulnerable loner. It goes without saying that he was incomparable when he seemed most like himself. His way with a line made movie dialogue part of the collective memory: 'I remember every detail. The Germans wore grey. You wore blue.' And a generation of men grew up scrambling his directions to Sam. Bogart's silences were also memorable. He didn't have to say anything. He didn't have to do anything. Well, maybe a whistle now and then. A little went a long way: that glance in his eyes before he covered the sentimental tracks with a caustic wink; or the movements he made with his finely shaped hands as they cupped the flame of a match for Mary Astor's cigarette and her eyes wandered up to his eyes, and his fingers traced the curve of her cheek across her lying lips, and two people were never so close. It was a relationship he was to share with his public until his death.

HEDY LAMARR

MGM, 1940
Photographed by LASZLO WILLINGER

When this 'new' glamour portrait was taken to announce her part in
Boom Town (MGM, 1940), the Viennese actress Hedy Lamarr, then
aged twenty-seven, was reckoned by general consensus to be one of
the most beautiful women in movies. This was true almost from the
moment she made her film debut in Germany in 1931. Of course
Hollywood cleared up any outstanding confusion by instantly labelling
her 'the most beautiful woman in the world', and after her American
screen debut in *Algiers* (1938) few would have disagreed. Her beauty
took people's breath away. When Sylvia Sidney was originally offered
the more dramatic role of the other woman in the film, she wisely
refused, for as she herself pointed out, there wasn't much chance that
people were going to notice anybody else after they saw Lamarr.
Sadly, *Algiers* was not only Lamarr's celebrated debut, but also the
high point of her American career for the next ten years, until Cecil B.
DeMille – the only man in Hollywood who seemed to understand what
to do with her – cast her as the Philistine temptress for his biblical
saga, *Samson and Delilah* (1949). They had been under contract to
different studios before then, however, and it was now almost too late
to save her career. During her years at MGM, the challenge, the
opportunity her mesmerizing appearance offered as a catalyst – if not
for art at least for compelling drama – was continually fumbled.
Confronted by a priceless object, everybody wanted her, but having
got her they were at a loss to know what to do next, which may have
been why the powers at MGM kept casting her as kept women,
repeating her first successful role until inspiration might strike. When
she wasn't kept, she was being miscast – as a Russian street
conductress; as the 300th actress to play Tondeloyo, the copper-
toned African man-killer; as 'Sweets' Ramirez, a fiery Mexican fish-
cannery worker . . . Her innate elegance, her sophisticated beauty, not
to mention her Viennese accent, made nonsense of them all, and,
inadvertently, began to provoke laughter. Though she was a good
actress (she had, after all, been first discovered by the theatrical
genius Max Reinhardt), Lamarr was incapable of transcending roles
and films which only her beauty made interesting. If her career proves
anything (and it spanned over twenty-five years, her last role being
that of a troubled movie star who seems to suffer the same miscasting
that plagued Hedy, in *The Female Animal*, 1958), perhaps it is this:
launching a thousand ships on the strength of beauty is an impressive
feat, but without a Homer to dramatize it few would ever have known
about it, and what's worse, fewer still would have cared. In the movie
business, Homers were even harder to come by than Helens.

ANN SHERIDAN

Warner Brothers, 1942
Photographed by ELIOT ELISOFON

One day, long after her heyday, Ann Sheridan was praised as being one
of Hollywood's great glamour girls, at which she kindly but firmly told
her enthusiastic admirer: 'That's not glamour you're talking about
honey, that's a sweater. I never had the glamour that Dietrich had, or
Crawford did. Dietrich, that was glamour! I was just a well-dressed,
well made-up motion picture actress.'

The Texan-born redhead who so described herself, was training to
become a teacher when her picture in a 1933 newspaper contest
brought her to Hollywood. She was a down-to-earth gal, who slowly
but steadily progressed from bit parts to small roles and then to leads
in numerous B films when luck, and a lull in her studio, made her the
industry's sensation of 1938 as the latest 'Love Goddess', heavily
publicized as the 'Oomph girl'. For the next decade, she was one of
the most photographed and recognized film stars (she had great
difficulty keeping a straight face while having to be seductive for her
portraits); though few of her roles, or the films she carried, were as
good as she looked, or the clothes she wore, her sympathetic work
kept her popular. She fought for better roles and wittily pooh-poohed
her 'mysterious oomph' as the sound of a fat man bending to tie his
shoelaces. Her roles all had the same things in common: good sense, a
sympathetic nature, warm looks and attractive sincerity.

GENE TIERNEY

20th Century-Fox, 1942
Photographed by FRANK POWOLNY

An exotic classy beauty, she signed with 20th Century-Fox and made her film debut in 1940, aged twenty, as the female lead in *The Return of Frank James*. The studio was not famous for its shrewd handling of the careers of its women stars, though at one time or another it had some of the greatest under contract. Its vehicles are better remembered for the director or writer; miscasting was rampant, and it is surprising that some stars lasted as long as they did. A few, like Gene Tierney and Tyrone Power, even survived to star after they left the studio. It took personal pressures, nervous breakdowns and lengthy spells in sanitariums, to halt Tierney's career. Her appeal which intrigued from the outset, and never totally disappeared – even when it could do little more than lurk behind roles that required her presence as an *objet d'art* – surfaced on several unforgettable occasions: in *Shanghai Gesture*, as the dissolute Poppy; in *The Ghost and Mrs Muir* (who else could be so believably in love with a ghost?); as the celebrated *Laura*, and in her finest hour and a half, as a woman who thought the world well lost for love in *Leave Her to Heaven*, a role and a vehicle that suited her to perfection.

She also worked for an enviable number of great directors: Fritz Lang, John Ford, Josef von Sternberg, Ernst Lubitsch, Otto Preminger, Rouben Mamoulian, John M. Stahl, Michael Curtiz, Edmund Goulding, Joseph L. Mankiewicz and Clarence Brown. Although her roles were not very often pivotal to their subject, and only a few of her films are among these directors' best remembered works, it all adds up to the intriguing enigma that was this woman's great attraction.

VERONICA LAKE

I Married a Witch, Paramount, 1942
Photographed by ELIOT ELISOFON
Costume by EDITH HEAD

Veronica Lake, the tiny, peek-a-boo blonde bombshell, here posing in her favorite costume for René Clair's classic *I Married a Witch*, was only twenty years old when this portrait study was taken. Her beguiling, biting, scampish witch (released from the trunk of a tree by a freak lightning storm, she returns to upset the household and descendants of the man who had her burnt a few hundred years earlier) was a role that suited her to perfection: she was a spry, punchy little cockerel from Brooklyn – breeding ground of other feisty spirits such as Clara Bow, Barbara Stanwyck, Mae West and Susan Hayward – whose beauty hid brains, and whose brains worked fast to seize a chance and make the most of it. She also had an explosive temper which she unleashed on those bigger than she, in size and power, resulting of course in the destruction of her career. But in her youth these qualities lent her an electric current that switched a lot of people on.

In her tough and bitter autobiography, written many years after her film career had ended, Veronica Lake spared few, including herself, and gave vent to her bottled rage at having been wasted by the system she bucked and the kind of films she was forced to make as a result. But to the end of her brief life, during which she defiantly kept hacking her hair short, she retained her passion for living, and drinking, and people not afraid to give as good as they got. There was also the fond memory of a few films: *This Gun for Hire*, *The Blue Dahlia* (which co-starred her with Alan Ladd), and especially Preston Sturgess' *Sullavan's Travels* (Paramount, 1941) and René Clair's film (which inspired one of the sixties' popular TV comedy sitcoms, *Bewitched*). It was her performances for Sturgess and Clair, the two great comedy directors of her era, which showed that she was more than a pretty face. These films came early on in her meteoric career, while Americans were almost as preoccupied with the way her long, soft hair fell so wickedly over one eye as they were with the war overseas. Veronica resented being known for her hair, but fame draws on strange things to single out one person for the attention of others: with Bette Davis it was acting; with Crawford it was staring; with Hayworth it was dancing and with Lake it was hair. But regardless of the gimmick that drew us to her, it was the unrepeatable quality within which made a star like Veronica Lake imitated and loved – not for what she may have thought she could do, but for the fact that she was there to do it at all.

ALAN LADD

Paramount, 1942
Photographed by HAL A. McALPIN

Ladd, the blond, soft-faced but steely-purposed actor, was one of the forties' great fantasy heroes, a sort of contemporary Galahad. Once he was set on his course, nothing could deflect him or cause his face to express any tell-tale emotion; being keel-hauled, punched-up, lashed or branded, never got him to show his hand. His stoic acceptance of physical abuse – well, maybe a wince here or there – may have been due to his limitations as an actor, but such subsequent gluttons for punishment as Kirk Douglas, Burt Lancaster, and Brando (the greatest masochist of them all), all more massive than Ladd and built to stand punishment, didn't improve on his performance though they suffered more visibly.

Alan Ladd (born 1913, died 1964), was one of the biggest box office stars of the forties and well into the fifties. In 1952, the same year Marilyn Monroe was selected by *Photoplay* readers as the movies' most popular actress, Ladd – who made his film debut in 1932, and ten years later scored a sensational breakthrough to superstardom as the ice-blooded killer in *This Gun For Hire* (1942) – was picked as the most popular male star. Actually, though he played his last role in *The Carpet-Baggers* (1964), his career began to peak soon after winning the award. Serious praise for his performance in *Shane* (1953) may have been the turning point. Loading fantasies with worldly honors tends to shatter the dreams we build around stars far more severely than gossip, bad publicity or even bad films.

Much has been made of his height, or lack of it, but this was never a hindrance in his heyday (before he put on fat) when his perfectly proportioned – head to neck, shoulders to hips, legs to arms – trim 5′ 5″ frame was ideal for his two-fisted dynamos, especially teamed with Veronica Lake, the 5′ 2″ pocket-Venus. They made a cool, crunchy duo in five films requiring no suspension of belief as they fought and won. The people surrounding them did not make them look small; on the contrary, Ladd and Lake made them look gross.

His actress/agent wife, Sue Carol, survived him, and one of his sons, David Ladd, became a successful child actor, while another – Alan Ladd Jnr – has gone on to be a major film producer, for a time president of 20th Century-Fox.

JAMES CAGNEY

Captain of the Clouds, Warner Brothers, 1942
Photographed by SCOTTY WELBOURNE

From the first, the Brooklyn-born Irish-American streetwise star rocketed across the screen with fire – a fire that remained undimmed until his voluntary retirement thirty years later. If acting can be called an art, then a part of Cagney's art was as an actor. It would certainly be the easiest and most direct way to understand his great success as a film star. Yet his powerful presence, his great reputation and his lasting contribution go deeper than his success as an actor or a dancer, although these disciplines, by husbanding his energies, offered a safety valve to protect him from burning out too soon. Nor was his achievement affected by occasional miscasting, which is another way of saying that he allowed his interpretation of a role to take the upper hand over his own personality. Herein lies the crux that separates the actor from the star: the one interprets, the other creates. Cagney, the actor, is excellent in *A Midsummer Night's Dream*, and even in Saroyan's *The Time of your Life*, but in both he is less than Cagney, the star.

Cagney, whose energy gave him a panerotic sexual magnetism, was the sparsest of performers, his grasp completely under control of his reach, his body's physical deficiencies – height, looks – so well integrated in the service of his work, that no one ever questioned his stature. The physical equal of any man larger than himself, he would not have seemed ill-matched opposite Gary Cooper, or have been a romantically less desirable partner for a woman like Rita Hayworth, although neither man nor woman could ever claim total credit for his motivations. As with an avalanche, nothing was able to stop him once he was aroused, and no one even thought to try. Cagney's force had focus, its path was consciously selected, and while nobody outside him could see the final destination, he had one. Finally, at the bottom of his valley, he stopped, retired and disappeared from sight to become a gentleman farmer. Essentially he was a great soul that no boundaries of time or taste could encompass. Cagney may have been a little man but he was never 'a little fellow'. He was his own work of art and as such we honor him.

INGRID BERGMAN

Warner Brothers, 1942
Photographed by SCOTTY WELBOURNE

In one of her two films when on loan to Warner Brothers, *Saratoga Trunk* co-starring with Gary Cooper (the other being *Casablanca*, co-starring with Humphrey Bogart), Bergman bests a smug little lawyer at his own game. Having agreed to her terms, he withdraws, but before leaving her presence he looks back seeing her as if for the first time, statuesque, smiling 5′ 10″ of youth and joy and beauty, and approaches her saying, 'Madame . . . may I say . . . you are very beautiful.' To which she replies with the laughter that fills her cheeks with bloom and radiates her countenance, 'Yes, I know. Aren't I lucky.' This luck she shared with the public that adored her first in Sweden, where she began her film career in 1934, and subsequently in Hollywood, to which she came under the Selznick banner to make her debut in a re-make of one of her Swedish hits, *Intermezzo* (1939).

She twice won the Oscar as Best Actress, for her roles in *Gaslight* (1944) and *Anastasia* (1956) and once as Best Supporting Actress for *Murder on the Orient Express* (1974). At one point her popularity was so high she was revered as a saint, only to find herself hounded and pilloried as a sinner when she met, fell in love with, and bore a child by the great Italian director Roberto Rossellini (working on their first film together, *Stromboli*, 1949) while still married to her first husband. She and Rossellini made five features and one short film together; these were initially received with scorn but have since become classics. Once sense again prevailed, her public, remembering the good times, returned in droves to re-establish a career the like of which, for duration and popularity, is something very rare, and testifies to her appeal as a woman. In 1980 she wrote one of the more charming film-star autobiographies, *My Story*, in which her candor, reflecting all that one had loved about the star, did nothing to diminish the appeal that has survived to the present.

PAULETTE GODDARD
and JOHN WAYNE

Reap the Wild Wind, Paramount, 1942
Photographed by EUGENE ROBERT RICHEE

Paulette Goddard's fame as a star rests on the two films she made with her husband, Charlie Chaplin, (*Modern Times* and *The Great Dictator*) and the three films she starred in for Cecil B. DeMille. *Reap the Wild Wind* (Paramount, 1942), which co-starred her as a Scarlettish Louisiana belle to John Wayne's brawny deep sea diver (in love with her sister), was the second of these. A feisty, realistic brunette, she began her film career as a blonde chorus girl in the early thirties, and though she never became one of the great archetypes, she was still a very popular leading lady, whether as Bob Hope's comedy foil, or as a pleasing addition to any number of forties wartime comedies and melodramas. She used her box office pull to enable Jean Renoir to make the excellent *Diary of a Chambermaid*, and had her biggest personal success as *Kitty*, a facetious Regency beauty.

By 1942, Wayne had leapt to stardom, after ten years as a B-Western hero, via John Ford's classic *Stagecoach*. He continued to be one of the most sought-after leading men for Hollywood's female superstars, until he himself became a movie legend through a series of cavalry Westerns directed by his friend John Ford. A man of heroic size with a powerful stance and an unblinking stare even when looking into a gun barrel, Wayne's lack of pretensions about himself or his popularity elevated him to the larger-than-life proportions he embodied so well in his films. When dying of cancer, he accepted his death with the same courage that had endeared him to his fans, who judged him not by his politics but by his nature.

BETTY GRABLE

20th Century-Fox, 1941–2
Photographed by FRANK POWOLNY

Betty Grable, the 'Pin-Up Girl of World War II', was the movies' equivalent of American fast food classics like Pepsi, Popcorn and Hamburgers. Her corn-blonde hair, polished pink cheeks, wall to wall smile and 'million dollar legs' made her the fighting forces' sweetheart. They made one of her many hundred bathing suit poses – most of which were taken by Frank Powolny – into the most famous pin-up in the annals of photography. Her films were formulas – color, songs and happy-endings – and through them she became the most consistently popular female star of the forties. Her stardom was an industry triumph; yet attempts, either by her own studio or others, to emulate the package with look-alike blonde doll-faces were at best moderate successes, which proved, if anything, that while she may have been in the right place at the right time, the mold she fitted was a glove no one else could wear.

GARY COOPER

Souls at Sea, Paramount, 1937
Photographed by MAC BULLOCH

There are stars and superstars, and then there are the handful by whose success one may understand the nature of the movies' massive appeal to the public. One of these rare people was Gary Cooper. He had appeared in over fifty bit parts when he made his mark on the screen as the shy, love-stricken cowboy in the 1926 Western saga *The Winning of Barbara Worth*, and for the next thirty-six years remained one of its most enduring heroes, the quintessential view of themselves that Americans wanted the world to see.

Souls at Sea, the last of his films for Paramount, where he had been under contract since 1926, was intended as that studio's rival to MGM's hugely successful *Mutiny on the Bounty* (1935). But the heavily cut version finally released was a routine picture saved only by Cooper's nonchalant, languid presence and his physical beauty, which had made him so effective in romantic and adventure films from the start.

Overleaf

ROBERT TAYLOR

TYRONE POWER

for *Stand By For Action*, MGM, 1943
Photographed by ERIC CARPENTER

for *Crash Dive*, 20th Century-Fox, 1943
Photographed by GENE KORNMAN

Robert Taylor (born 1911), son of a country doctor, made his film debut in 1934. Tyrone Power (born 1913), son of a famous matinee idol, made his film debut in 1932. Their careers ran along similar lines over the same span of time: Taylor's at MGM, Power's at 20th Century-Fox. Both suffered from the backhanded blessing of their good looks which made them ideal casting for the romantic heroes but also led critics to disparage their abilities. Taylor, a modest man with few pretensions, accepted his fate and brought a charming dignity to his roles. Power, from a strong theatrical background, took the jibes more personally and tried throughout his career to escape the 'pretty boy' tag. To be fair, their studios did try to broaden their appeal to include men, though they were unwilling to risk the fans both men had made in films like *Lloyds of London* (Power, 1937) and *Camille* (Taylor, 1937). Thus Power was cast as a gangster in *Johnny Apollo* (1940) and Taylor played one successfully in *Johnny Eager* (1942). Metro gave Taylor a lavish production for *Billy the Kid* (1941), and 20th did the same for Power in *Jesse James* (1939), both romanticized portraits of these Western outlaws that appealed to men and women alike.

By the end of the forties, their great romantic vogue was behind them; Tyrone Power branched out in parts he found more taxing (though his fans always preferred him romantic), while Taylor played the roles his studio gave him, and was the perfect incarnation of *Ivanhoe*, *Quentin Durward*, Lancelot in *Knights of the Round Table* and a Roman commander in the time of Nero. When Power died suddenly of a heart attack in the midst of filming *Solomon and Sheba* (1958) – a return to the sort of roles he is best remembered for – he was already winning serious recognition for his acting. Taylor, who continued in films and TV until shortly before his death in 1969, received recognition through succession: a new generation of romantic stars, cast in roles similar to those he had played in the past, made everyone remember how much better he and Power had been.

BETTY HUTTON

Paramount, 1944
Photographed by BUD FRAKER

Betty Hutton was the frenzied 'blonde bombshell' of loud and lively forties' musicals. She was already established on Broadway as a big band vocalist when she burst onto the screen in *The Fleet's In* (1942) in a supporting role that stole the show with a shredding, mike-bending, epileptic rendition of 'Arthur Murray taught me dancing in a hurry'. For reasons best left for psychiatrists to sort out (she was really quite pretty and in her quiet moments even moving), the bulk of Hutton's screen characters behave like furies at a sale in their stampede for a bargain place in the sun. It was a personality 'schtick' she had in common with a lot of these big-voiced, big-hearted over-dramatic songbirds of the forties – Martha Raye, Judy Garland (Danny Kaye and Jerry Lewis were their male counterparts) – who shared her romance with embarrassment. Be that as it may, Hutton kept herself just this side of self-caricature and for ten years starred in hugely popular films until the time came when her temperamental outbursts off-screen were more troublesome than her on-screen image was profitable, and she left films, vanishing almost as suddenly and dramatically as she came. Unlike Garland, she never found a new audience in her attempted comebacks. In her ten years as a Paramount star, Bud Fraker shot most of her portraits, and one can be sure that she drowned out any noise the pistols might have made.

FRED ASTAIRE

Ziegfeld Follies, MGM, 1946
Photographed by ERIC CARPENTER

Ziegfeld Follies, the star packed, Technicolor musical spectacle, was MGM's third movie using the great showman's name, and their first no-story musical since *The Hollywood Revue* of 1929. It was also supposed to be Fred Astaire's swansong since he planned to retire afterwards. His last few films had not been that successful, and his box office prominence was on the wane; it had been difficult to find a new partner the public would accept with him or roles that suited him as a solo performer, and other actors, among them Gene Kelly, were ready to take his place even though none could fit his shoes.

Ironically it was his last-minute replacement for Gene Kelly, who had cracked an ankle, that led to his triumphant return to the screen two years later as Judy Garland's partner in *Easter Parade* (MGM, 1948). This led to some of the most memorable musicals in Hollywood's last years: *The Bandwagon, Funny Face, Silk Stockings* and *Barkleys of Broadway*, which re-teamed him for the last time (and only one in color) with Ginger Rogers. This shot of Astaire, tap-tapping a bongo rhythm to the understandably awestruck gaze of the male chorus line, is from a scene that was cut from the over-long *Ziegfeld Follies* and is possibly of Fred singing one of his own songs, 'If Swing Goes, I Go Too'.

LINDA DARNELL

in costume for *Hangover Square*, 20th Century-Fox, 1945
Photographed by GENE KORNMAN

At 20th Century-Fox where the female stars were mostly decorative furniture, Linda Darnell, under contract from 1939 to 1952, made a marvelous Edwardian *chaise-longue*. She was featured or starred in a great number of costume and adventure dramas that would have been all right without her but gained enormously from her participation. Perhaps the only performer with American Indian blood in her veins ever to become a star, Darnell was very pretty, and developed into a voluptuous beauty whose perfect complexion was always an asset as she made the transition from virginal heroines in mantillas and lace to women not averse to revealing a tough streak beneath the deceptive sweep of their wardrobe. Like many of the popular stars during the contract system, her career tailed off as soon as she left her studio's fold, but her popularity in her time had been real enough and would have been the same had she worked for any other studio. Her success was the result of a system which produced a lot of films, needed a lot of stars and offered the public a large selection from which to choose their favorites. Darnell had been a very popular choice.

FRANK SINATRA

CBS, 1945
Photographed by TED ALLAN

Brooklyn-born (1915) Francis Albert Sinatra actually made his first screen appearance while a singer with the Tommy Dorsey Band in Eleanor Powell's 1942 musical *Ship Ahoy*, and it was as a romantic crooner that he rose to astronomical heights in the early years of the War. Riot police were called out to control the screaming, hysterically weeping mobs of young, boyless bobbysoxers whenever 'The Voice' performed. Naturally, he was deemed to have film star possibilities, and after a couple of false starts (not that unusual since nobody has ever really solved the problem of presenting pop idols with a film image the first time around), which began with *Higher and Higher* (1943), he was signed by MGM and immediately topbilled in fluorescent musicals like *Anchors Away*, *Take Me Out to the Ball Game* and *On the Town*. Since, when not singing, the cadaverous-looking little baritone cut a decidedly less-than-romantic figure, he was often teamed with the athletic dancer, Gene Kelly, and lost the girl. He also lost the girl when he wasn't teamed with Gene Kelly. And the one time he got the girl, as *The Kissing Bandit*, nobody came to see him. Either way – though in private his romantic life was more fruitful – his floundering film career began to undermine his popularity as a singer, and in the early fifties his headlines were neither as singer nor actor but as the husband of the Love Goddess, Ava Gardner. By 1952, he was considered washed up; his film career was in a shambles and he was dropped by MCA, the giant talent agency. They were all wrong! He returned triumphantly, not only as the pre-eminent popular song-stylist of the century, but as an Academy award-winning film star for his performance in *From Here to Eternity* (1953), which led to his new guise as a ring-a-ding-ding swinger who got all the girls. Thirty years later, his fame is enormous, his wealth untellable, his influence (extending from casinos to The White House) unbelievable, and his social status on a par with princes and presidents.

ROY ROGERS and TRIGGER

Republic Pictures, 1940s
Photographed by ROMAN FREULICH

Freulich, a great stills photographer at Universal since the twenties, left there in 1945 to become head of the portrait gallery at Republic Pictures – a studio that actually had none of the great glamour stars, but most of the hugely popular heroes of children's Saturday matinees, the Western stars, protectors of the purple sage. Foremost among them was a likeable smooth-skinned singer named Leonard Slye, who started out in films in 1935, and by 1942, renamed Roy Rogers, was universally agreed to be 'King of the Cowboys'.

Rogers, and his best pal, Trigger (the smartest horse in the movies), rode in a pre-Freudian West, where bad was black and good was white and the hero always won the fight: no problem arose that couldn't be corralled and branded in sixty minutes, allowing time out for several campfire songs, and a promise of more with a happy sunset fade-out. The appeal of these movies was not to the big city audiences, but to children and the broadly based rural population whose support proved a telling reminder of the fundamental source of the American filmgoing public. While better publicized stars came and went, these forerunners of the subsequent Country and Western explosion went on and on and on ... Then, in an ironic recapitulation of a favorite Western theme – the displacement of the little man by the big landowners and railroaders – the small budget family Western, which had begun as a cottage industry neglected by the major studios, found itself shunted aside as the big companies and the big stars decided the time was right for them to move in. Roy Rogers, Gene Autry and Co found themselves replaced on the big screen by John Wayne, James Stewart and Co. But the West that Roy Rogers exemplified in his films was a never-never land far removed from the complex, macho-orientated world which directors like John Ford, Howard Hawks, Anthony Mann and others now made of the last frontier – where a man could be a man only at a price. Their sunsets were tinged with a different sort of nostalgia; innocence was gone from this West, and the end of the day brought one inevitably back to the problems of the present. Reading the writing in the sky, Roy had already moved Trigger and the rest of his corral to the new pastures offered by TV in the early fifties and, with his series, continued as one of the great heroes of a new generation of children.

PAL

as *Lassie*, MGM, 1946
Photographed by CLARENCE SINCLAIR BULL

In the highly competitive dog-eat-dog world of Hollywood, nobody ever said an unkind word about Lassie, one of its greatest stars. In his long and distinguished career, C.S. Bull photographed most of Metro's great stars – Garbo, Lamarr, Harlow, Gable, Jeanette MacDonald to mention only a few – but Lassie was the only dog. Even though most people in the profession knew her shameful secret and could have destroyed her career, no one said a word. Lassie was no bitch; she was a he named Pal.

The star of seven films about an adventurous bitch, Lassie was first played by Pal, who, like his four successors in the role, was a male, since in the animal kingdom, the male, though less deadly, is usually more beautiful than the female of the species. He was acclaimed for his performance in the first of the series, *Lassie Come Home* (MGM, 1943), and had one critic enthusing over him as 'Greer Garson in furs'. After his film career ended, he found long-running success in a TV series based on the collie's further exploits. In 1978 he tried for a screen comeback in *The Magic of Lassie*, but it just wasn't there.

LAUREN BACALL

for *The Big Sleep*, Warner Brothers, 1944
Photographed by SCOTTY WELBOURNE

Betty Joan Perske, who gave men the licence to whistle, was blessed by nature with two advantages: the personality of a buddy and the look of a *femme fatale*. This combination initially took the nineteen year old actress to the top with her first two films made in 1944 – *To Have and Have Not* and *The Big Sleep* – scoring a success even the deadpan expressions of a Buster Keaton could not undermine. It helped, of course, to be co-starred in them with Humphrey Bogart who fell in love with her during shooting, and to have Howard Hawks, who deliberately set out to prove that he could make her a star, directing her every move in the same totally controlled way von Sternberg had done with Marlene Dietrich. Things were not so simple when she was on her own: for a long time she was better known as Humphrey Bogart's wife, and as the unmemorable co-star of a number of unmemorable films. She nevertheless had a marked talent for survival and, many years later, after her success on Broadway and her jolly autobiography, she has become heir to our memories of the truly memorable stars of the forties, and, in her own way, one of them.

Overleaf

BURT LANCASTER, LIZABETH SCOTT and KIRK DOUGLAS

I Walk Alone, Paramount, 1947
Photographed by BUD FRAKER

A triptych for the crime drama, *I Walk Alone*, co-starring three of producer Hal B. Wallis' recent film finds: Burt Lancaster, Lizabeth Scott and Kirk Douglas. Both Lancaster and Douglas, who co-starred in a number of films over the next two decades, were famous for tough exteriors hiding sensitive natures. Lizabeth Scott, who appeared in films with one or the other, though never again with both together, was less versatile. Like Lauren Bacall and Ella Raines (other actresses in the Veronica Lake mold), her career revolved on the archetypal vamp foundations: a bone, a rag, a hank of hair, and a voice that sounded as if it had been buried somewhere deep and was trying to claw its way out. The film's plot had ex-convict Lancaster seeking revenge on nightclub owner Douglas who had cheated him, while Miss Scott was a singer whose song 'Don't Call It Love' pretty well stated her case as one who felt misunderstood and left out. The physical similarities of the three made the roles interchangeable and the plot hard to follow – which perhaps is why it has become a classic of the *film noir*.

CARMEN MIRANDA

for *A Date with Judy*, MGM, 1948
Photographed by VIRGIL APGER

Carmen Miranda, known as 'The Brazilian Bombshell', was the original Chica Chica Bum Chic gal of forties musicals – a large swash of Rousseau on the movie screens, a festive explosion of outrageous razzmatazz that may not have added much to culture but did add a lot to one's enjoyment of it. Everything about this happy demon (except her height) was larger than life: her behavior; her conondrums with the English language as it tripped its way into her head and out through her mouth in accents thick and hilarious; her eyes as they shrank into slits and lost themselves behind her cheeks rising and swelling through the effort required to enunciate her tongue-twisting lyrics at rapid speed; the continual motion of eyes, mouth, shoulders, hips, arms, hands, fingers and feet, the latter supported by elevated platforms that heightened her appeal, and the ever more extravagant gowns that have inspired nightclub performers ever since – garlands of sequins, bowers of living blooms around her hips and breasts, and orchards of fruit growing out of her turbans. The total effect was that of some medieval fertility ritual goddess whose presence was a promise of fruitfulness.

Carmen Miranda (born 1909) was a Portuguese singer raised in Brazil, where she made her film debut in 1933. She arrived, inevitably, in Hollywood just before the outbreak of War to do a specialty number in one film, *Down Argentine Way* (20th Century-Fox, 1940), almost stole the show and stayed to star in Technicolor musicals for the duration. Had she been any less than she was, the embarrassment might have been excruciating, but fortunately she was way way over the top – like an inspired cartoon character come to life – and one could sit back, relax and enjoy her. Her vogue was over by the end of the War, though she kept making sporadic film appearances between stage and TV work until her untimely death in 1955. This portrait of her, in one of her costumes, dates from this later period. Clearly she had not changed – only the times had. But who said the fifties were fun?

JENNIFER JONES

Selznick Productions, 1946
Photographed by JOHN MIEHLE

David O. Selznick gave roles to a number of women that made them spectacular stars: Vivien Leigh and Olivia de Havilland in *Gone With The Wind*; Joan Fontaine in *Rebecca*; and Ingrid Bergman, who started her American career under his guidance, in *Intermezzo*. Such lesser but still popular players as Guy Madison, Rhonda Fleming and Rory Calhoun also began with him. He wanted to make a young actress named Phyllis Isley, whom he renamed Jennifer Jones, his greatest success. As Pearl, the half-breed heroine of his wild and beautiful masterpiece *Duel in the Sun*, she was a marvelous overwrought minx, and the star he had hoped for: they were married. A neurotically self-obsessed, other-worldly quality about her fitted her perfectly for Flaubert's *Madame Bovary* and King Vidor's *Ruby Gentry*, and opened a host of possibilities to her: as a candidate for sainthood in one film, a troubled ghost in another, a tormented bride in a third, and a string of sexually frustrated, frustrating women who tantalized but never bored their audience. She was too complex to be bottled; her quirky mannerisms and unusual beauty retained their ability to keep one guessing and hoping for the role that would bring all the strands together, and produce the movies' most absorbing case study of twentieth-century womanhood.

GLENN FORD

Columbia, 1946
Photographed by ED CRONENWETH

Glenn Ford – seen here in his home – was to Rita Hayworth as Jon Hall was to Maria Montez, which is not to say he was Gilbert to her Garbo. But he had a sexy line in handing out hairshirts to women, giving them a bad time for having had a good time before they knew him. At 6' 1" he was taller than he looked on the screen (usually it's the other way around), probably because of his deceptively cuddly demeanor.

LUCILLE BALL

as the ringmistress in the Merry-Go-Round number of *Ziegfeld Follies*,
MGM, 1945
Photographed by ERIC CARPENTER
Costumes by HELEN ROSE

Lucille Ball doing her statuesque showgirl bit for the opening number
of this tasteful revue. The controlled contrast between carrot-topped
Lucille in her candy-pink gown and the pantherettes dressed with
thousands of minute black sequins, made this one of the film's more
eye-catching sequences.

Lucille Ball (born 1911), in pictures since 1933, might have been
permitted a twinge of *deja vu* as she whipped the chorus into shape,
for twelve years earlier she was on the other end of the whip as a
blonde chorine chained to an auction block for one of Busby
Berkeley's wilder and weirder musical fantasy numbers in *Roman
Scandals*. Ball's look of wry, bemused detachment stood her in good
stead during her years of second string glamour-puss parts and
comedy foils when she regularly found herself drawn into situations
against her better judgement, only to have her misgivings come true.
The screen's foremost female clown, she never blamed anyone but
herself for her mishaps – an endearing quality even if it doesn't always
make stars, as Eve Arden (a similar actress in similar roles) also found
out. But Ball's elastic features were a caricaturist's dream as her
already high cheekbones became accentuated even further when her
mouth pursed into thought and her eyebrows rose to her forehead to
make a visible question mark of her interior doubts. On film, Lucille
rarely embarrassed anyone, though she was forever being
embarrassed. Ironically, she became a superstar on TV, in the
immensely popular *I Love Lucy* series, when she reversed roles;
instead of hapless accomplice she became the instigator of zany
farcical escapades. It was the mark of her brilliant comedy timing that
she could remain a lovable madcap and avoid deteriorating into a
freakish caricature. Her success was her triumph.

MERLE OBERON

as *Lydia*, United Artists, 1941
Photographed by BOB COBURN

Bob Coburn and Merle Oberon both joined Samuel Goldwyn at about the same time, in 1935 – she to become the popular Americanized leading lady of Goldwyn's films, he to be the man in charge of the stills department and head of the portrait gallery. In their respective roles, Coburn and Oberon worked together over the next ten years, even after both left Goldwyn, and produced many expert examples of Hollywood glamour. This costume portrait is further enhanced by the use of color that emphasizes her jasmine scented beauty amidst the rich black-blues of the backdrop, her pleated blue-tinged organza ballgown and the jet black of her hair.

Merle Oberon, the durable Anglo-Indian beauty, born Estelle Merle O'Brien Thompson in Tasmania (1911), made her film debut as an extra in a 1930 British B film, but soon her dramatic, if one-dimensional, beauty caught the eye of the Hungarian-born British producer Alexander Korda, who groomed her for stardom and was her husband for a time. In 1935 he sold a half-share in her contract to Samuel Goldwyn, another famous star spotter, who oversaw her transition from exotic to all-American. Never a top star, but a popular actress in a number of prestigious films, Oberon continued to make periodic starring appearances until her death.

GREGORY PECK

*1945 portrait for *Duel in the Sun*, United Artists, 1946*
Photographed by MADISON LACY

Gregory Peck in character as Lewt McCanles for David O. Selznick's barbaric, sprawling, overwhelming Western epic *Duel in the Sun*. The picture was taken in the first months of shooting. Lewt was a bad man, all bad, but he was also very sexy and cool, and knew how to laugh and have a good time. Peck, whose screen reputation was founded on playing good, honest, Godfearing men, has always insisted that he was not comfortable playing the part, which offered one of the few touches of color in a distinguished but almost monotonously similar career.

Selznick was a master chef. Although he had many brilliant men working for him, his extraordinary gift as a producer was in giving the semblance of unity to an end that was the sum of the parts of so many assorted talents. King Vidor directed long chunks of this film, as did William Dieterle, Josef von Sternberg, Otto Brower, Reeves (Breezy) Eason and Chester Franklin among those known. *Duel in the Sun* is Hollywood studio filmmaking at its most delirious: awful and splendid.

MARLENE DIETRICH

Paramount, 1947
Photographed by A.L. 'WHITEY' SCHAEFER

This portrait stems from the glamorous forty-seven year old star's Hollywood comeback period. She was again at Paramount (the studio where her phenomenal American career had begun its ascent in 1930 with a series of luminously beautiful films directed by Josef von Sternberg), to star in *Golden Earrings* as a wily sooty-faced gypsy fortune-teller who helps an allied soldier to outwit the evil Huns. It wasn't much of a film, but it was a job, and like so many other returned soldiers, she got down to work and made the most of it. Her next film, *A Foreign Affair*, put her back on top.

GLORIA GRAHAME

RKO, 1948
Photographed by ERNEST BACHRACH

The archetypal American southern belle was the British Vivien Leigh. The quintessence of the supersophisticated American about town was the British Cary Grant. And the personification of American fast-talking humor is the British Bob Hope. But who would have thought that the star whose face springs into mind when one thinks of the *ne plus ultra* of the American *film noir* – its fallen-blonde, pouty lipped sinful-eyed angel – would be the British actress Gloria Grahame? It all goes to show that whatever makes a star looks after the rest; and that our notion of how seditious American man-traps should look and purr owes a lot to the novels of Raymond Chandler, who never got over being educated in Britain. Be that as it may, nobody else was *quite* like Gloria Grahame – glittering with the barely controlled fires seething beneath the social veneer. While she herself was no criminal, her presence alone could incite men to criminal actions if only to attract her attention as she prowled big city streets – so sultry, so spiteful, so wanton, and so lethal if the mood took her and the man didn't. She was the great bitch goddess, shedding her coats like snakes their skin, and tugging at the tight coils of her hair to conjure up a world of bedrooms in disarray. Her freezing looks were as memorable as her scalding actions, and whether she had made only one film like that or fifty she would still have made her niche. (Fortunately she was in several including *The Big Heat* and *Human Desire*.)

   This 1948 portrait predates her tight-curled poodle-cut fifties' image, but Bachrach was too good not to focus attention on the twenty-three year old actress' strikingly individual looks, which barely condescend to fit in with the lush colors and silken fabrics designed as trappings for up-and-coming *femmes fatales*. Silk or sack, her clothes are only worn to be torn; for her all things are black or white, and anarchy is the roost she rules.

CARY GRANT

The Bishop's Wife, Goldwyn Productions, 1947
Photographed by ERNEST BACHRACH

In *The Bishop's Wife*, Grant played a bishop's guardian angel who comes to earth when the bishop has financial problems. The film co-starred Loretta Young as the bishop's wife and David Niven as the troubled prelate. Harps being synonymous with angel's work, the idea for this photo could not have been hard to come by but must have been fun to do.

As with Garbo and Dietrich, Garland and Monroe, almost anything one can say about the man is superfluous. He too was one of a kind: magical, durable, a symbol of the sort of filmmaking that rekindles memories and on reviewing makes one realize that the emotions were justified.

RITA HAYWORTH

for *The Loves of Carmen*, Columbia, 1948
Photographed by BOB COBURN

The casting of Rita Hayworth as Carmen, the passionate Spanish gypsy who rolls her own cigarettes and picks her own men, was inspired; the film, *The Loves of Carmen*, was not. Bob Coburn, one of the best portrait photographers in the business was head of the stills department at Columbia. His job was not just to supply a steady stream of attractive pictures of the studio's stars, but also to get the public hungering for their appearances. Since more was expected of a Hayworth film than of anyone else's, he and Rita worked harder than usual to make the stills come alive.

Although by this time Rita's mind was on the Riviera, where she was about to embark on the great romantic adventure of her life, she was also the total professional and knew that the stills in the gallery were her last chance to carry out some of her hopes and ideas for the film role; in a sense these stills were another part of her job. Since here there were no directors or writers or long schedules to interfere it was all up to her and her sympathetic confidant behind the camera. This perhaps explains why, when the memory of a film's failure has faded and a still from it re-appears somewhere years later, it retains the power to rekindle the desire to see the film again and hope that this time it will come out as good as we thought *she* was.

ALIDA VALLI

Selznick Productions, 1947
Photographed by JOHN MIEHLE

Alida Valli, who made her film debut in Italy in 1936, is here
photographed after being brought to Hollywood by David O. Selznick
for the *femme fatale* lead of the starry *The Paradine Case*, a
courtroom murder drama directed by Alfred Hitchcock and originally
purchased by MGM as a vehicle for Greta Garbo. Valli – her American
billing – was one of the first of the postwar Italian stars to arrive in
Hollywood, where her intensely brooding, velvety personality and
looks were expected to make her a new Garbo or Bergman at the box
office. That she became neither in no way hindered her from
continuing one of the longest starring careers in the European cinema,
and appearing in such classics as the Italian *Senso*, and the English *The
Third Man.*

LOUIS JOURDAN

Selznick Productions, 1947
Photographed by JOHN MIEHLE

Replacements for Charles Boyer were as scarce and sought after as Garbo's, and postwar Hollywood was always on the look-out for continental types to fit the bill. Few were as strikingly handsome as the then twenty-eight year old French actor whom Selznick also introduced to American audiences in *The Paradine Case*, where he was the extra-marital spur to Alida Valli's murderous wife. Like her, Jourdan never achieved anything near the success hoped for with American audiences, as his roles quickly became stereotyped and his romantic beauty something of a handicap in an era of postwar realism. Dividing his career between films and TV in America and on the Continent, he co-starred in two classics of the forties, Max Ophul's *Letter from an Unknown Woman* (Universal, 1948) and Minnelli's *Madame Bovary* (MGM, 1949), but scored his greatest personal success in the romantic 1958 musical *Gigi*.

ELIZABETH TAYLOR

MGM, 1949
Photographed by HYMIE FINK(?)

Elizabeth Taylor, London-born (1932), American-raised film star in a portrait taken about 1948–9. When still in her teens, she was reckoned to become the most celebrated beauty of her generation. Since making her screen debut in a 1942 comedy, *There's One Born Every Minute*, her life seems to have been played out before the cameras. At its peak, her career brought her two Oscars (one for *Butterfield 8* – while not very good, she was never more beautiful than when she dug her stiletto heel into Laurence Harvey's toe – and one for the overblown theatrical *Who's Afraid of Virginia Woolf*); the highest fee ever paid an actress up to then, for her ill-fated film about the ill-fated *Cleopatra*; five husbands; and a reputation fit for a Jacobean heroine – as homewrecker, heartbreaker, jetsetter and lavish spender. She shocked, but never lost the interest of the public who, above and beyond it all, admired the spectacular will to live, which enabled her to overcome several close brushes with death, and the fact that she took her failures in the same broad stride as her successes, as part of life's *grande bouffe*.

While her film roles drew primarily on her camera-proof looks to provide the stimulus (at their most spectacular in her twenty years as an MGM star), even her success in dramatic roles borrowed a great deal of its effect from the surprise that a girl who had everything should feel it necessary to show talent too. As Kate, Shakespeare's mouthpiece for the liberated Renaissance woman in *The Taming of the Shrew* (1967), her potential for housing harridans and angels under the same fair skin had its perfect vehicle. In close-ups her camera-wise face conveyed the eloquence, wit and understanding of Shakespeare's text. It may well have been her finest moment.

ROBERT RYAN

for *The Set Up*, RKO, 1949
Photographed by ERNEST BACHRACH

Evoking so accurately the seedy, down-at-heel world of the professional boxer, *The Set Up* is rightly regarded as probably the best boxing film ever made. It was shot in black and white, as was the only other film on the sport to equal it, *Raging Bull* (United Artists, 1980), but this color shot of Robert Ryan as the washed-up prize fighter refusing to take a fall and seen here slugging it out with Hal Fieberling, nonetheless captures the merciless, stark, brutal quality of the film and its subject. This was one of Ryan's best roles and no doubt the fact that he had held his college heavyweight boxing title for four years enabled him to bring an even greater sense of authenticity to the part. It also provided Robert Wise with his directorial breakthrough after a period of routine B pictures, and won the Critics' Prize at the 1950 Cannes Film Festival.

ROBERT MITCHUM

RKO, 1948
Photographed by ERNEST BACHRACH

His nonchalant, laid-back stance appeals to men even though they lack his courage to defy convention, while his sleep-hooded eyes still challenge women to rouse him and make him their own. He is a man who, despite an apparent lack of interest, is clearly an actor. He has mastered his craft for, after almost forty years – most of them as a star – he can still make his films an event and is more often the only interesting thing about them. After years of drifting around, working at a succession of odd jobs – handyman, trucker, prize fighter (at which time he may have suffered the damage that accounts for his sexy, hooded look) and promoter for an astrologer – he got into movies in 1943, playing bit parts in some eighteen films, usually as a hood or a heavy, whether in B Westerns, wartime propaganda exploits or cheap jukebox musicals.

By 1948 he was already on his way to becoming one of the great stars; by 1956 he was one of the few remaining and yet even to the present day, when his face has taken on the contours of a pleasantly lived-in landscape, he remains the outsider, familiar but never fenced in – his eyes retaining their shrewd assessment of pretension and humbug. Those foolish enough to take him at first glance soon learn that, when it comes to the crunch, here is a man more than a match for anything they have to offer.

CYD CHARISSE

MGM, 1948
Photographed by ERIC CARPENTER

Tula Ellice Finklea was thirteen when she joined the American Ballet Russe company where she met her first husband and ballet instructor, Nico Charisse. Although she made her film debut in 1943 as Lily Norwood, it is as Cyd Charisse that we remember the American cinema's lyrical dancing beauty. A bonus to any film, a compliment to any arm, she blossomed as Fred Astaire's partner in the fifties' musicals *The Bandwagon* and *Silk Stockings*, and in several films dancing opposite Gene Kelly, most memorably *Singing in the Rain*.

Before she found her niche in musicals, MGM, where she was under contract for most of her film career, tried to fit her into a variety of roles which kept her career in a rut despite her beauty. This was partly due to an emotional detachment, not uncommon among classically trained dancers but of limited appeal to the general public. The sensitivity and eloquence of character she projects as a dancer found little echo in her roles as housewife or vamp. It was in the studio's last burst of great musicals that she came into her own and then her remoteness lent added significance to her roles: Galatea thawed out and became real when wooed by Astaire in scenes masterminded by Vincent Minnelli. This mythical transformation elevated her to cult-like status among European admirers, and her popularity was great, if not so pretentious, in America.

LEX BARKER and CHIMP

as TARZAN and CHEETAH, RKO, 1949
Photographed by ALEX KAHLE

Lex Barker was the tenth of the sixteen actors to don the loincloth of
the jungle superman created by Edgar Rice Burroughs, and in five films
made between 1948 and 1952 became the best remembered actor to
play the part after Johnny Weismuller. Since *Tarzan* is one of popular
literature's superstars, playing him in a successful series inevitably
reduces the rest of one's career to that of 'The man who played . . .'
While the ivy league Alexander Crichlow Barker Jnr never escaped
the tag, he at least managed to pick up another one, on the Continent,
as the star of another popular German-made series based on one of
that country's legendary heroes, Karl May's *Old Schattermand*, and, in
between, as the husband of two of Hollywood's more glamorous
Janes: Arlene Dahl and Lana Turner.

JANE RUSSELL

Paramount, 1948
Photographed by A.L. 'WHITEY' SCHAEFER

Jane Russell, photographed while on loan-out from Howard Hughes to co-star with Bob Hope in the Western comedy spoof *The Paleface* (1948), only her third film since she had begun in 1941.

A tall tawny brunette, Jane Russell was famous long before her first movie was ever released: posters of her for Howard Hughes' Western *The Outlaw* had created a censorship crisis, and the film – in the works since 1941 – was only released to the public in 1949. They should have known better by this time, but still flocked in droves to see what all the fuss was about, only to discover that the movie itself was a tame affair compared to the posters. In most of these, a full length Rabelaisian wench lolled on banks of hay, toyed with a straw in her mouth and cast truculent glances over her high up-rearing breasts – breasts which, by nature and Howard Hughes' aeronautical designs, were the cause of all the uproar. With teaser lines like 'How would you like to tussle with Russell', and 'Name two good reasons why Jane Russell is a star', it was easy to think the lady in the picture was the outlaw of the title. In fact, the film concerned Billy the Kid and another male friend, but nobody could remember who played Billy the Kid. When Schaefer shot this portrait, he could afford to frame her face in a furry hood and forget her body, since by this time any photo of Jane Russell brought the rest of her shape to most people's mind. Jane Russell was in fact a much more talented lady than the initial image suggested, and had an active and popular career in films well into the fifties as a woman who had seen a lot and was not about to be surprised by much.

GRETA GARBO

MGM, 1941
Photographed by CLARENCE SINCLAIR BULL

If there is nothing left to say about Greta Garbo, there are still a few things of interest about this portrait taken when she was thirty-six years old. It revealed the new 'Americanized' Garbo for what would be her last film, *Two-Faced Woman* (MGM, 1941). Bull by then had photographed her for twelve years, achieving some of the most compelling portrait studies ever made. Yet the unique quality of this photograph, from their last session together, comes from the facts which surround it: it is one of only two known color portraits ever taken of her during her career (the other was Bull's shot of her in character as *Camille*); it is also a generic rather than a costume study, since her role was that of an Americanized playgirl in a contemporary comedy. Aided by hindsight, we can now sense a weariness and lack of interest behind the older yet still beautiful face, and this must have made it easier for her to retire when the film itself flopped and her new contract with the studio failed to provide the incentives to make her stay on.

MONTGOMERY CLIFT

1949–1950
Photographed by HYMIE FINK

He was beautiful, very, very beautiful. And he was sad, vulnerable, and prone to melancholy; a boy not yet a man. Though callow in *Red River*, a cad in *The Heiress* and a coward in *A Place in the Sun* – three of his most famous films, made one after the other in his first three years in Hollywood (he made his debut as a sensitive soldier in *The Search*, 1948) – there wasn't a woman in the audience who did not love him and want to look after him, and they made him an immediate and sensationally big star.

It was because of his enormous appeal to the matinee crowd that Clift's acceptance as one of the great originals (Brando's forerunner in behavior and manner without the mumbling), was so late in coming; after a car accident midway through the filming of *Raintree Country* smashed up his good looks, his performances were always highly praised. He died of a heart attack in 1965 at age forty-five. Twelve years later, his biographers revealed him to have been drugged, gay, lonely and tortured, but this fitted in with the current image of doomed heroes and he became a legendary figure in the same mold as Monroe, Dean and Presley.

AVA GARDNER

Generic art for *Pandora and the Flying Dutchman*, Romulus Films, 1951
Photographed by TED REED

Death or the nunnery: in her most memorable roles Ava Gardner seemed predestined for one or the other. Her powerful appeal takes its resonance from western civilization's unstated obsession with death, and the implicit understanding that certain people – the beautiful, the passionate, the headstrong, or the too truthful – are chosen to be sacrificed for the rest of us. In this lies much of Garbo's appeal as well, but what gives Gardner's personality its own distinction is the wonderful gusto with which she lives life while it lasts, leaving it without regret when the time is up. In all her finest films, she possesses this sense of destiny: *Snows of Kilimanjaro, Pandora and the Flying Dutchman, The Barefoot Contessa, The Killers, Showboat*, and *Knights of the Round Table*.

Ava Gardner, the actress, often spoke of her dissatisfaction with her roles; the star could have had no such complaints, since the camera singled her out and made the rest superfluous. At the peak of the excitement surrounding her in the early fifties, somebody, searching to pinpoint her appeal, dubbed her 'The World's Most Beautiful Animal', and watching Gardner stride free and panther-like with sure and flawless gestures, was one of the movies' great attractions. Her beauty, like that of Rita Hayworth, was never an end in itself but only a means of reflecting the woman within.

For such a dynamic, mythic screen personality, Gardner's career was surprisingly spotty. Like so many of the great stars, she made most of her films before her image had come into focus. There were too few afterwards: she grew older during her long absences, returning in roles that disappointed by their lack of opportunity for her. And yet the effect was still there even when she was no longer the same beauty. One example suffices: in her cameo role in *The Life and Times of Judge Roy Bean* (1972), John Huston fades the film out on a close-up of Gardner reading a letter from an admirer she has never met, and fills the screen with her face until it blends into the light. The moment, through its use of her, tells us everything about reality and dreams, and the need for legends if life is to be renewed and death lose her sting.

Ava Gardner was born in North Carolina in 1922. The daughter of a poor tenant farmer, she found herself with an MGM contract in 1940 after a photograph of her landed in their casting department. Her screen debut was in a bit role. She has been married several times, and her private life has been foodstuff for the international press.

LANA TURNER

MGM, 1952
Photographed by ERIC CARPENTER

Taken a dozen years after the first study, this archetypal Hollywood glamour portrait still shows Lana Turner as the consummate star: done up to the nines, the look suggesting intimacy, the shoulder promising bacchanalia and a white fur rug to lie back upon. It was the sort of photograph Hollywood turned out by the thousands, and it brightened the pages of magazines, and made a lot of people go to the movies. Yet to achieve its effect took a great deal of skill. The photographer had to know his subject well; he needed to capture the look which was inviting to one half of the audience without being offensive to the other half; he had to get the lights to flatter his subject and enhance the mood. The result, when it succeeded, sprang from teamwork that could stretch over a decade or more. Eric Carpenter and Lana Turner started their careers at MGM almost simultaneously: he as an upcoming portrait photographer, she as a new girl on the lot. While Turner remained with the studio, Eric Carpenter shot more stills, portraits, pin-up and glamour shots of her than anyone else. It was the kind of working relationship, typical of those existing throughout the studios, which produced the images and films that established Hollywood's supremacy in the world of movies. This psychological edge over other countries and their stars survived even after the American studio system had collapsed.

MARILYN MONROE

20th Century-Fox, 1953
Photographed by GENE KORNMAN

The best known, most representative image of Marilyn Monroe in her American Love Goddess phase. Kornman was not interested in interpreting her or understanding her; his job was to enshrine her. The result is a photograph which belongs with the Garbos by Clarence Sinclair Bull, the Crawfords by George Hurrell and the Hayworths by Bob Coburn. What these women achieved in such a moment made everything leading up to it, and everything that happened afterwards, subjects of interest.

Kornman started taking gag shots in the early part of the century. He was Harold Lloyd's portrait and stills man all through the twenties and until Lloyd ceased production in the early thirties, when Kornman went to the newly formed 20th Century-Fox. Together with stills and portrait photographer Frank Powolny, he took all the portraits of the studio's stars until his retirement in the sixties.

JOAN CRAWFORD

Queen Bee, Columbia, 1955
Photographed by BOB COBURN
Costume by JEAN LUIS

During the seventies, feminists argued that Hollywood had conspired over the years to hold back the emancipation of women by feeding them seductive, dishonest images of woman happy in her role as man's subordinate. It was a shortlived argument, as political theorists were confronted with the facts. Hollywood, in its most influential period, the thirties, was the great twentieth-century matriarchal preserve, dominated by images of strong-willed, self-made female stars: Davis, Stanwyck, and Garbo; Dietrich, Hepburn and Crawford. Nothing weak about Crawford! The story of her own life, her rise from poverty and chorus lines to the pinnacle of fame (never mind those of the career women she played so forcefully in almost half a century as a star) riddles this theory with more holes than a Swiss cheese. Whatever Crawford did to get ahead, she did knowingly; whatever her characters suffered, sacrificed and achieved in the course of the story – from *Letty Lynton* to *Mildred Pierce*, from *Mannequin* to *Queen Bee* – they were aware. And while the heroines in some of her early films may have given up their achievements in the competitive world for love, their choice was hardly dictated by necessity, given the quality of the men they settled down with (eight films co-starred her with Clark Gable). From the mid-forties onward, her image became too powerful for male stars to risk obliteration by supporting her, with the result that her co-stars became interchangeable. The continued willingness of her heroines to settle down at the fade-out had less to do with love than with the difficulty of finding good escorts and unpaid staff – marrying them gave her the control she needed and an acceptable solution in a society which allowed any number of permutations in private as long as the conventions were upheld in public. Crawford was strong. Until 1953 all her films were in black-and-white; they had enough drama without color. *Queen Bee* was one of the last of her high-powered vehicles, and there was little rosy dew left on this chrome-plated job. Could a way have been found to harness the power she ran on, there would have been no oil crisis.

She was born Lucille Fay Le Sueur, in Texas in 1904, and made her film debut at the newly formed MGM in 1925, after stints as laundress, waitress, shopgirl, hostess, and hoofer in a Broadway chorus. It was in the same year, through a competition in the pages of *Movie Weekly* offering $1,000 for a suitable name, that out of thousands of replies Joan Crawford – a name that she made a synonym for Hollywood Glamour – was found. From that time until her death in 1977, her greatest single loyalty was to her fans. She was a hypnotic actress from the start, but almost at once set out to make herself something much more challenging – by turning her life into a work of art. As such, she provided a role for other actresses to play, and at the same time removed herself from the race.

JAMES DEAN

Warner Brothers, 1954
Photographed by BERT SIX

Like a latter-day rock star, Dean reluctantly poses for a publicity shot.
His barely concealed irritation at having to do such sessions was
merely part of a greater resentment toward all that the studios stood
for as powerful corporate entities.

   James Dean was a furious cry against the cloying, smug hypocrisy of
a consumer society in the fifties. While we shall never know if he was
capable of providing any answers, since he died so tragically young, it
was enough that he voiced and portrayed the frustrations and
discontent brewing in the American youth of his time. Their
identification with him led to his instant and enormous success in
three films – *East of Eden*, *Rebel Without a Cause* and *Giant* – made in
just over one year. His premature death in 1955, when his car crashed
in a race, was itself a tragic statement of his dissatisfaction and ensured
his elevation to legendary status. So strong and clear was the message
he expressed in his own time that today, thirty years later, along with
Monroe and Presley, he still embodies the spirit of a society in search
of its identity – a search unleashed in the sixties, and never
satisfactorily resolved.

KIM NOVAK

Columbia, 1955
Photographed by BOB COBURN

In the days when the major studios dominated Hollywood, it was said that they were the creators of stars. Yet in virtually every instance in which a studio decided to launch a mogul's favorite, placing all of its resources behind her, the results were laughable. MGM's Louis B. Mayer gave his personal go-ahead to Ginny Simms and Lucille Bremer; Goldwyn struck out with Anna Sten and Sigrid Gurie; Daryl F. Zanuck, of 20th Century-Fox, made stars of Arlene Wheelan(!), Virginia Gilmore(!), and Bella Darvi(!); Republic Pictures' President Herbert J. Yates staked his studio on the success of Vera Hruba Ralston(!); and Columbia's power-broker Harry Cohn was forever telling his biggest star, Rita Hayworth, and the rest of the industry, that he could make anyone a big star whenever he wished. His attempts had included Patricia Knight, Adele Jergens and Janet Blair, but not until 1954 was he able to prove his point. Cohn found a twenty-one year old Polish-American brunette model named Marilyn Novak, an athletically built woman with large expanses of white skin who, as 'Miss Deepfreeze', had been touring the country showing how refrigerators worked. He had her overhauled from stem to stern – her figure slimlined, her hair a new champagne blonde. Then he ordered the stills department to produce reams of glamour portraits (deliberately imitating Rita Hayworth's poses) and shipped them out by the ton to whoever might find them useful. He renamed her Kim Novak, and after a few bit parts in flops nobody realized she had made until after she became a star, she was officially unveiled in *Pushover* (1954). Apparently the trick worked: by 1956 she was America's no 1 box office attraction. True, Monroe was in New York and out of the running for the moment; Ava Gardner, Lana Turner, and Rita Hayworth were by then working as highly paid freelance stars; and Kim's only real rival with a similar hard-pitch sales campaign behind her was MGM's Elizabeth Taylor (in 1980 the two would co-star as aged stars in *The Mirror Crack'd*). But, there was no denying that audiences liked Novak and did go to see her films, so long as she was co-starred opposite the top male names in the business: Fred MacMurray, Frank Sinatra, William Holden, Tyrone Power, Jeff Chandler, or James Stewart. She did have a hot come-on sort of look, and a frozen don't-touch-me demeanor – giving her what one of her directors described as the appeal of 'the lady in the parlor and the whore in the bedroom' – looking cool, lush and marvelous in lilac as she walked through her films expressing polite interest and a terror of emotional reactions toward the situations which arose. By the early sixties her phase was over, but she had certainly proved that Harry Cohn could make a star and, twenty years later, fans of fifties' movies are still enamored of her.

JAYNE MANSFIELD

for *The Girl Can't Help It*, 20th Century-Fox, 1956
Photographed by FRANK POWOLNY
Dress by TRAVILLA

A movie star is somebody the public wants. Jayne Mansfield was
nobody because there was already Marilyn Monroe. In the wake of
Monroe's success, Hollywood teemed with imitations. This, in itself,
was not an unusual phenomenon; what was extraordinary was the
number of imitations. Not only every studio but also every country
came up with one. England had Sabrina and Diana Dors; France sold
Mylene Demongeot in that image and, of course, Bardot. Germany
came out with a series of teutonic, pneumatic blondes like Barbara
Valentine. Back in Hollywood, Universal came up with the clone-like
Mamie Van Doren, Columbia with Cleo Moore, Warner Brothers with
Carole Baker, Paramount with Anita Ekberg, MGM tried with Barbara
Lang, and on and on ran the list of actresses who found themselves
poured into the mold. Even Sophia Loren and Tina Louise were, in a
manner of speaking, off-shoots of the 'steamy' Marilyn in *Niagara*. No
single studio was as determined to dredge up replicas as Monroe's
own lot, 20th Century-Fox, who found the most extravagant
pretender in Jayne Mansfield. Although none of the Monroe copies can
be said to have made it in that guise, none tried harder (right up to her
freak death in a car crash) than Mansfield. She had always wanted to be
an actress and being married at sixteen and a mother at seventeen had
done nothing to quench this ambition. Considering the physical
attributes for which she will always be remembered, it was not
surprising that one of her earliest stunts to get into the papers was to
participate in the publicity drive for a Jane Russell picture. Russell
herself had shaken her pneumatic image and wasn't bothered by
anybody wanting to fill that void. Though Mansfield worked in a
succession of busty bits at various studios, it was the Monroe
phenomenon which changed her from brunette to blonde, and made
her play down her high IQ to dumb-blonde level. Her breakthrough
came with the 'Monroe'-inspired role of the blonde sex-bomb in
Broadway's *Will Success Spoil Rock Hunter?* The display of her
physical wares represented a personal triumph which led her back to
Hollywood in 1955 where she became a star for Fox, who were
looking to curb Monroe's power. But it never again happened for
Mansfield. During the next nine years she played the same role again
and again and again, and when the parts being offered by American
studios dried up, she worked in low-budget European films, some of
which co-starred her with her husband of the moment, muscleman
Mickey Hargitay. Her death in 1967 came near the end of a one-track
career. Clearly her own failure was a reflection of the studios' failure:
they could not fob off an imitation onto the public. Jayne Mansfield's
tragedy was not lack of talent or personality but a false image which
dwarfed and defeated both.

ELVIS PRESLEY

MGM, 1957
Photographed by VIRGIL APGER

1956: The hottest name to burst upon the entertainment world – Elvis Presley, 'Mr Rock and Roll' – arrived in Hollywood. His manager had signed him to a sensational contract that divided his services between three of the major studios – 20th Century-Fox, MGM and Paramount – all of whom were desperate to find a product that might recapture the gigantic youth market they had lost. Presley's popularity had taken off a few years earlier, and gained additional impetus every time another tirade was unleashed from parents and pulpits, symbols of the established authority which reacted with outrage every time Elvis gyrated his hips to a song. They saw the man and his music as an incitement to undermine the morals of their young. But the fifties' youth – safe, secure and stagnating – were starved for heroes of their own, idols who would reflect their preoccupations and be their signal, the way earlier stars had been for their parents. Having found what they wanted in James Dean only to lose him so suddenly, they fastened onto Elvis and wouldn't be moved. Elvis 'The Pelvis', owner of 'Blue Suede Shoes' and keeper of the 'Heartbreak Hotel', was a generation's public declaration of its ignored needs. This contemporary idol made his film debut amidst clamorous publicity in 'the story he was born to play', set in the Civil War era a hundred years before his time. Elvis, idol of the masses, was the bashful boy who lost the girl and died at the end!

1969: Elvis starred in his thirty-third Hollywood film, playing a priest, and nobody cared. By now he was a sad, nearly spent shadow of his former self. Age wasn't to blame. Films had done that to him. The movies he made, none of which ever captured the charisma of his live performances or created a framework that would have accounted for his appeal, had drained him, pulped him, put him through a blender and made him as smooth and bland as Bing Crosby. Although some of his early films were all right, and even successful because of his record following, he was out of date the moment the Beatles and Rolling Stones appeared on the scene.

Elvis had to return to the stage, and new records, to recapture some of his old public, who by now were no longer kids while Elvis was only a Liberacied version of his old self. By the time he left Hollywood in 1969, most of the major entertainment stars were the product of the record industry. When Elvis died, the world mourned the death of the King of an Era. Few mourned the film star.

MARLON BRANDO

as *One-eyed Jacks*, Paramount, 1961
Photographed by BUD FRAKER in 1960

Marlon Brando posing for poster art for *One-eyed Jacks*. Finished in 1959, re-shot in 1960, released in 1961 and forgotten in 1962, this 2½-hour Western was noticeable for its stunning scenery, including shots of the sea – not often does one get to see the sea in a Western. Brando, starring in his only directorial effort to date, was unusually co-operative when it came to promotional ideas for selling this film, which may be how this sort of untypical action still of him came about. He was notoriously unco-operative when it came time to pose in the studio gallery for publicity portraits. Like many other highly publicized failures, the film has developed a cult following over the years.

MARILYN MONROE
and JANE RUSSELL

as Lorelei Lee and her best friend, Dorothy,
in *Gentlemen Prefer Blondes*, 20th Century-Fox, 1953
Photographed by FRANK POWOLNY

Jane Russell's lack of ego and Monroe's sense of fun meshed perfectly
when they co-starred in Anita Loos' light-hearted satire of the old
adage that when a woman goes bad, men go right after her.

   The film crowned Monroe in her position as the nation's new Love
Goddess with the promise of many sparkling hits to come, and Jane
Russell's career continued, with less fanfare, but very successfully for
several more years. *Gentlemen Prefer Blondes* was one of the last
lavish, lush, Technicolor musicals the studio shot in the old, standard
screen 1.33:1 ratio, because the same year, in an effort to combat the
crippling inroads TV was making on the box office, 20th Century-Fox
revived a French-patented wide-screen process and named it
Cinemascope. After the success of their first film, *The Robe*, with the
new 2.35:1 aspect ratio, they used it for all their other films. At the
same time they went from Technicolor to Eastman Kodak, which was
easier and cheaper to process and needed less light when shooting.
Unfortunately, its shortcomings have become only too apparent, since
the colors have failed to remain true and durable with the passing of
time. The same cannot be said of the stars.